www.wadsworth.com

www.wadsworth.com is the World Wide Web site for
Thomson Wadsworth and is your direct source to
dozens of online resources.

At *www.wadsworth.com* you can find out about
supplements, demonstration software, and student
resources. You can also send email to many of our
authors and preview new publications and exciting
new technologies.

www.wadsworth.com
Changing the way the world learns®

D1532133

Current Perspectives
Readings from InfoTrac® College Edition

Terrorism and Homeland Security

Second Edition

SABINA L. BURTON

University of California, Irvine
California State University, Fullerton

Australia • Brazil • Canada • Mexico • Singapore • Spain
United Kingdom • United States

THOMSON

WADSWORTH

Current Perspectives: Readings from InfoTrac®
College Edition: Terrorism and Homeland Security, Second Edition
Sabina L. Burton

Senior Acquisitions Editor: *Carolyn Henderson Meier*

Assistant Editor: *Jana Davis*

Editorial Assistant: *Rebecca Johnson*

Technology Project Manager: *Susan DeVanna*

Marketing Manager: *Terra Schultz*

Marketing Assistant: *Jaren Boland*

Marketing Communications Manager: *Linda Yip*

Project Manager, Editorial Production: *Iris Sandilands*

Creative Director: *Rob Hugel*

Print Buyer: *Linda Hsu*

Permissions Editor: *Kiely Sisk*

Production Service: *Ruchika Vij, Interactive Composition Corporation*

Cover Designer: *Larry Didona*

Cover Image: *Photolibrary.com/Photonica*

Cover and Text Printer: *Thomson West*

Compositor: *Interactive Composition Corporation*

Thomson Higher Education
10 Davis Drive
Belmont, CA 94002-3098
USA

For more information about our products, contact us at:
Thomson Learning Academic Resource Center
1-800-423-0563

For permission to use material from this text or product, submit a request online at
http://www.thomsonrights.com.
Any additional questions about permissions can be submitted by e-mail to
thomsonrights@thomson.com.

Library of Congress Control Number:
2005937225

ISBN-13: 978-0-495-12994-3
ISBN-10: 0-495-12994-1

Contents

III. DOMESTIC TERRORISM   43

IV. ISSUES IN HOMELAND SECURITY   63

Preface

The U.S. Department of State defines terrorism as "premeditated, politically motivated violence perpetrated against noncombatant targets by subnational groups or clandestine agents, usually intended to influence an audience." We distinguish between "domestic" and "international" terrorism depending on the geographical origin of the perpetrators. Domestic terrorism describes acts committed by American citizens directed at American institutions or members of the government, private businesses, or general population. International terrorism involves the activities of foreign individuals or groups either on American soil or abroad. The most infamous act of international terrorism to date took place on September 11, 2001, when al Qaeda members under the leadership of Osama Bin Laden attacked the twin towers of the World Trade Center in New York City, while the devastating bombing of the Murrah Federal Building in Oklahoma City was of domestic nature. Terrorism experts further categorize terrorists as nationalistic or religiously driven, state-sponsored, left- or right-wing, or anarchistic in nature.

In the last two decades, the international stage and its main players have changed significantly. With the collapse of the Soviet empire, we gladly welcomed the end of the cold war, its hateful propaganda, and the lingering threat of a third world war. Especially in Europe, citizens were reminded daily that peace was fragile and expensive. Knowing that the European continent could not survive the outbreak of a nuclear battle, the superpowers resorted to political and economic sabotage, aggressive espionage, and the strategic use of terrorism. It was an open secret that the KGB financed terror groups like the deadly Red Army Fraction in Germany, arranged their training in Palestinian camps, and offered safe havens on communist ground after successful hits against the democratic system. Western nations, on the other hand, generously supported Afghan fighters against the Soviet Union and Iraq's Hussein in his war against Iran. Nonetheless, the terroristic threat seemed more manageable and predictable than today. Neither NATO nor the Warsaw Pact allowed terroristic groups to follow their own agendas. Today we face more uncertainty than ever before and are adjusting slowly to a multitude of hot spots.

The Oklahoma City bombing and the World Trade Center attacks have taught America that terrorism can no longer be considered a foreign problem. Premeditated and carefully planned acts of violence have been used around the world to express dissatisfaction with a government and the distribution of wealth, to sabotage and weaken a system or paralyze its leaders and citizens with fear. Whether the actors are politically motivated, religious fanatics, or environmental or animal-rights extremists, this form of terror has become the preferred method of "persuasion" for those who lack legitimate purpose, logic, and reason.

The many faces and multiple causes of terrorism, however, cloud its definition. Terrorists may be viewed as freedom fighters by those sympathetic to their cause. The controversy about terrorism, fueled by motives in the middle-eastern region, ethnic and national differences in Eastern Europe, and conflicting economic and political ideologies in Western Europe, Japan, Latin America, and the United States, has greatly impaired an international assessment of the terroristic threat. Even close allies cannot agree on a strategy to fight terrorism as we have seen in the wake of 9/11.

Put together to complement Jonathan White's *Terrorism and Homeland Security*, this reader includes articles from Thomson Wadsworth InfoTrac College Edition to reflect the current discussion of terrorism in the news media. Like the main book, the reader is divided into four parts, the criminology and controversy of terrorism, international terrorism, domestic terrorism, and issues in homeland security.

The first set of articles attempts to understand and define the phenomenon of terrorism. In a "A Global Definition of Terrorism," the authors state the importance of developing uniformity in accepted concepts of warfare that focuses on perpetrators, state sponsorship, motive, method, loss threshold, and actor. An agreement on these basic ideas will enable better information gathering and a more accurate prediction of future terroristic activities.

"The Root of American-Style Terrorism" points out that homemade terrorism requires a different assessment than international terrorism. It is caused by the psychopathic traits of the perpetrators and not by fanatic political or religious ideology. The American terrorist, just like the typical disgruntled citizen mass-murderer, is driven to make a public statement, however, not to voice his upset with American politics but rather with the frustrations and failures he had encountered in his personal life. We are dealing here with a pathetic loner with an antisocial personality disorder whose deadly potential could be averted with early detection and intervention programs. "Who Is a Terrorist?" challenges our perception of terrorism. Would not our own founding revolutionaries have fit today's description of terrorists?

"Understanding Religious Terrorism" focuses primarily on Muslim-driven terrorism and explains the forces behind it: the reawakening of Islam in a modern world, the ongoing Israeli-Palestinian conflict and the international and especially American inability to resolve it, and the frustration of Arabs over their limited political voice due to authoritarian government and lack of political rights. The author urges the United States to strengthen and support moderate Muslims by an honest assessment of the Middle Eastern situation and long-term programs that provide a political and economic future for Arabs.

"Chosinness and the Theology of Terror" analyzes the religious fanaticism of terrorists. The relentless pursuit of destruction and hate is fueled by a conviction that God, who is their God alone, is supportive of their cause and means to achieve it.

Terrorism does not only challenge the political finesse of our government but also tests the willingness of our international banking system to properly deal with customers who use its service to finance their lethal objectives. "Controversial Customers; Financing Terrorism" reports on victims of terrorism who are now holding banks legally accountable for their financial involvement.

The next set of articles deals with international terrorism. "The Global Threat" warns that none of us, no matter what nationality or religion, are safe from terroristic attacks. One of the goals of al Qaeda is to isolate the United States and sabotage efforts for a global response to terrorism.

How do we address Islamic terrorism? The author of "The Struggle for the Soul of Islam" believes that we are powerless in curbing the forces that fuel radical Islamic terrorism, the hateful preaching against the West, and the promotion of martyrdom. For once, we do not have influence on or even access to these extremist teachers, nor can we in good conscience restrict their efforts in this country without violating our constitutionally guaranteed freedom of religion and speech. Again, the key to diminishing the threat lies with the moderate Muslim community. The West must actively encourage and support the modernization of Islam to instill the true values of the Quran.

Much of the effectiveness of Islamic terrorists can be found in the willingness of its perpetrators to sacrifice their lives for the greater cause. "Who Are the Suicide Bombers?" examines the pawns in the deadly operations. The wire-pullers of terrorism recruit mainly the uneducated and poor and cleverly manipulate them into thinking their acts will provide them with a ticket to heaven.

Counterterrorism is facing a tougher battle of identifying potential terrorists as the article of "Europe Confronts Changing Face of Terrorism" points out. Al Qaeda has been recruiting willing "soldiers" in various countries and many of them, especially those in Europe, bring with them higher education and professional skills valuable to the terror network. The use of these individuals, many of them either born, raised, or educated in western countries, and who also possess their citizenship, make it difficult for law enforcement and intelligence to single them out and prevent them from perpetrating their vicious plans.

The last article in this group, "Masters of Suicide Bombing," does not let us forget that international terrorism is not owned by radical Muslims.

Whether it is the National Republican Army in Northern Ireland, the Basque Separatists in Spain, or the Sri Lankan guerrillas, terrorism shows its ugly face in many parts of the world. The Tiger fighters, as these terrorists are also called, have successfully copied the suicide missions of the Jihad. The target of their "humanitarian" effort of giving their lives to the cause, however, is not the common people but the army of Sri Lanka.

The third set of articles analyzes domestic terrorism. In "Homegrown Terror," the author describes the motivation, personality, and criminal act of a "typical" American terrorist. Educated and skilled, this terrorist has in-depth knowledge of chemical and/or biological warfare. Either a left- or right-wing extremist or a believer in anarchy, he—and sometimes she, when we are dealing with radical anti-abortionists, or animal or environmental activists—displays an antisocial personality. The media has regarded these individuals with curiosity and fascination, and up to 9/11 neither news reporters nor the State Department of Justice showed much concern over our own homegrown terrorists.

"The Growing Threat of Home-Grown Terrorism" attempts to correct that ignorance and points out that it is time to pay closer attention to a form of violence that has steadily increased in frequency and intensity. Eco-terrorists such as the Earth Liberation Front "gloat like Bin Laden" when they brag about their violent methods like tree-spiking, industrial sabotage, arson, and bombings—all in the name of Mother Earth. It may just be a matter of time before their targets become human.

In "America's Homegrown Terrorists" we take a glance at the futile attempts to reason with environmental and animal rights activists such as representatives of the Animal Liberation Front (ALF) and the Earth Liberation Front (ELF). While not intending to hurt any human life (at least not yet), both terror organizations openly admitted that their goal was to cause serious economic damage. The fact that ALF kidnapped and branded a British journalist in 1999 shows that only a very fine line has kept these terrorists on behalf of earth and animal from murdering people.

The fourth and last group of articles discusses homeland security issues. The author of "The Homeland Security Bureaucracy" critically reviews the structure and mission of the Department of Homeland Security (DHS) and questions its effectiveness in preventing future terrorist attacks. The article discusses the directorates, the department's missions, new priorities, critical tasks, and growing pains. The size of the department with its many heads may be less effective as an anti-terror measure than the government claims. Combining 22 agencies under one roof is a challenging task with questions of authority and proper delegation of tasks. It counters the community service effort of the last two decades of many local agencies to move away from large headquarters to make law enforcement more accessible to citizens.

More bureaucracy does not do away with bad bureaucracy. "The Controversy About U.S. Policies" informs the reader about mistakes made before 9/11 and the government's reluctance to learn from them.

Many scholars state that we are paying a high price to prevent future terrorist attacks on the United States: the erosion of Civil Rights by the USA PATRIOT Act. "The USA PATRIOT Act and Civil Liberties" discusses the sensitive task of guaranteeing individual rights while protecting the safety of the nation against terroristic threats. The article refers to the careful deliberation of maintaining a balance of power and liberty by former U.S. Supreme Court justice and U.S. prosecutor Robert Jackson in Nuremburg after World War II.

This reader is designed to present a collection of current opinions, evaluations, and studies on the topic of terrorism and further enrich the information presented in Jonathan White's fifth edition of *Terrorism and Homeland Security.*

I

THE CRIMINOLOGY AND CONTROVERSY OF TERRORISM

The recent acts of terrorism in the United States and abroad have taught us that an effective strategy against this form of warfare requires an international consensus on target identification and operational modus of enforcement.

The first challenge is to agree on a global definition of terrorism. In order to do so, the various forms of terrorism, and their roots, structures, and support systems need to be identified and outlawed.

1

A Global Definition
of Terrorism

Thomas A. Player Jr., Harold D. Skipper, and Janet Lambert

A s more countries adopt state-sponsored pools, the patchwork of terrorism definitions in their charters could multiply. If this occurs, the
potential for confusion and conflict intensifies, and commercial enter-
prises that operate across borders will find risk management increasingly complex. A global definition is not immune from political influence in certifying
an act of terrorism, but it is more likely to result in consistent application of
coverage and more predictable certifications of terrorist acts.

DEFINITIONS OF TERRORISM

In order to propose a global definition of terrorism, we must compare and
identify patterns in the elements that make up existing interpretations.

Perpetrators. All definitions of terrorism categorize the perpetrator, sometimes as a person or organization acting on behalf of a terrorist group or
on behalf of foreign interests. Although some definitions do not require
the individuals to be connected to an organization, most do. Few define
such persons as operatives of a foreign government, however, which
would bring the definition closer to that of war.

Risk Management, Sept 2002, v49, i9, p60(1).
"A Global Definition of Terrorism" by Thomas A. Player Jr.; Harold D. Skipper; Janet
Lambert. © 2002 Risk Management Society Publishing, Inc. Reprinted with permission
from Risk Management Magazine. All rights reserved.

State Sponsorship. State sponsorship generally is not a prerequisite in the definition of terrorism. None of the U.S. proposals for federally backed terrorism coverage include it, nor does the London market or the United Kingdom's Pool Re.

Motive. Definitions of terrorism routinely require motives for the actions. The U.S. proposals vary. Two proposals suggest destabilization of the government. Three of the proposals name "to coerce the civilian population" as a motive. Hong Kong's proposed ordinance broadens the motive to "intimidate the public and to require that the use of threat is made for the purpose of advancing a political, religious or ideological cause." The definition from Lloyd's Underwriters Non-Marine Association (NMA) adds as a motive "to put the public, or any section of the public, in fear."

Method. The major distinction between the various definitions' reference to method is the use of violence. The Pool Re definition requires an act of force or violence. In the U.S. versions, the act must be unlawful and cause harm or be violent. The Hong Kong proposal encompasses a broad definition of method that involves serious violence against a person; serious damage to property; creation of a serious risk to the health or safety of the public; or serious interference with or disruption of an electronic system or essential service, facility or system. International Underwriting Association and NMA definitions call for an act or a threat of an act.

Loss Threshold. Most definitions do not set amounts of loss in absolute terms. Rather, they call for serious loss of life and property. Two U.S. proposals, however, do require property losses in excess of $5 million before an act can be certified as terrorism. (This loss threshold is not to be confused with the point at which state-sponsored coverage begins.)

Certified and by Whom. To be considered an act of terrorism, some definitions require government certification. Both France and the United Kingdom require certification of an act of terrorism by government ministers. All U.S. proposals require certification either by the secretary of the treasury or the secretary of commerce.

A GLOBAL DEFINITION

Drawing from these components, we offer the following global definition of terrorism: An act, including, but not limited to, the use of force or violence, committed by any person or persons acting on behalf of or in connection with any organization, creating serious violence against a person or serious damage to property or a serious risk to the health or safety of the public, undertaken to influence a government or civilian populace for the purpose of advancing a political, religious or ideological cause. Such act shall be certified as an act of terrorism by the senior judicial or administrative official designated by the adopting government and shall not be subject to appeal.

Thomas A. Player, Jr. is chairman of the insurance and reinsurance group at Morris, Manning & Martin, LPP. Harold D. Skipper is chairman, professor and C. V. Starr chair of international insurance at Georgia State University. Janet Lambert is a partner with the reinsurance and international risk team at Barlow Lyde & Gilbert.

2

The Root of American-
Style Terrorism

Jack Levin and James Alan Fox

BOSTON—After the Sept. 11 attack on America and before the Washington-area sniper's killing spree, many Americans associated terrorism with violence perpetrated by Hamas, Al Qaeda, or Hizbullah. Yet the largest number of what the FBI calls "terrorist" acts in this nation have not come from the Middle East at all, but from our own citizens.

FBI statistics show there have been nearly 500 "terrorist" acts on US soil over the past two decades—the agency defines terrorism as the unlawful use of violence to intimidate or coerce a government or a civilian population. Most of these incidents involved Americans targeting fellow Americans.

Unlike terrorist acts committed in Latin America, Europe, or the Middle East, terrorism American-style arises more from pyschopathology than politics. The homegrown terrorist seeks to send a message—but not necessarily one about our national policy. He—virtually all are men—has usually led a life of frustration, failure, and obscurity; and he strives to tell the world, usually through the barrel of a high-powered firearm and occasionally with explosives, that he is an important and powerful individual. In a sense, he is playing God. And, certain unhealthy changes in our social environment encourage him to do so.

The typical homegrown terrorist, or mass killer, is socially isolated. He lacks the support systems that might have eased him through bad times and averted his devastating rampage. The most brutal and violent cases seem to be the most telling: In almost every mass murder, the killer suffers a loss that,

The Christian Science Monitor, Oct 23, 2002, p09.
"The Root of American-Style Terrorism" by Jack Levin and James Alan Fox. © 2002
The Christian Science Publishing Society. Reprinted with permission of the authors.

from his point of view, is catastrophic—typically the loss of a job in a bad economy, the loss of a good deal of money in the stock market, or the loss of a relationship as in a nasty separation or divorce.

To begin making sense of seemingly senseless murder, we must examine not so much the killer's biography or even biology, but our society itself. The clue to the American-style terrorist's motivation can be found in a disturbing social trend that affects almost everyone: the eclipse of community, a dwindling of the social relationships—family ties and neighborliness—that had protected former generations of Americans from succumbing to disaster. In an earlier era, family or neighbors could be counted on to assist in times of financial or social ruin; today, you're basically on your own. Many Americans simply have no place to turn when they get into trouble. Without options or support, murder can seem like the only way out of an out-of-control situation.

At the same time, growing numbers of Americans are opting for the solitude of telecommuting and the Internet. They avoid traffic jams on the highways, but also give up interaction with co-workers. Their neighborhoods no longer provide them with a source of friendship and camaraderie. Typically, Americans don't know their neighbors' names and faces—but they do know the e-mail addresses of faraway acquaintances they've never met face to face. We're quick to communicate at a superficial level with strangers in chat rooms, but too busy to sit down with our neighbors and share conversation.

According to our analysis of FBI homicide statistics over the past 20 years, areas of the country with large numbers of transients, newcomers, and drifters—destination cities often with relatively low unemployment rates or good weather attractive to those looking for a new beginning or a last resort—also have a disproportionate share of the nation's mass shootings.

So long as they remain back in Omaha, Rochester, or Boston, they can depend on their family, friends, and fraternal organizations for personal assistance. But when they reach destinations like Los Angeles, Chicago, Houston, or Washington, D.C., they find themselves very much alone. When times get tough, they have nobody around to discourage them from doing the wrong thing.

In other parts of the world, community continues to prevail. It would be all but impossible for a Londoner to move 1,000 miles for the sake of a job. In all likelihood, he'd wind up as an immigrant in Moscow or Rome, where both language and culture are discouragingly different. By contrast, Americans often move their residence hundreds, if not thousands, of miles—in most cases, not even crossing state lines. From a practical standpoint, then, mobility is no big deal.

In preventing future terrorists, like the Washington-area sniper, from committing desperate and despicable acts of violence, perhaps we should recognize the human misery and suffering of the isolated Americans in our midst—misery with no company. These are human beings who are very much alone in a psychological sense. They could use a helping hand, encouragement and support, a little understanding from their acquaintances, neighbors, and co-workers. In the end, these efforts may not totally rid our society of psychopathic terrorism, but would go a long way to restore the American community.

Jack Levin is the Brudnick Professor of Sociology and James Alan Fox is the Lipman Family Professor of Criminal Justice, both at Northeastern University in Boston.

3

Who Is A Terrorist?

A Toast to Moral Clarity; Were American Revolutionaries Terrorists?

Nicholas D. Kristof

I n the next step in the war on terrorism, we're likely in the coming months to invade Iraq in ways that will terrorize civilians there. So this holy season is a useful moment to step back and critically examine moral clarity, President Bush's byword, a concept that tends to stiffen the backbone of conservatives but make liberals fidget.

Is it fair to present the war on terrorism as a parable of good (us) versus evil (them)? Grenville Byford reflected the skeptics' view in a *Foreign Affairs* essay, arguing that moral clarity is more apparent than real and that "the sooner the rhetoric is retired the better." Highly nuanced intellectuals tend to poke three kinds of holes in moral clarity:

1. Terrorism is in the eyes of the beholder. President Reagan declared the African National Congress a terrorist group not long before its leader, Nelson Mandela, won the Nobel Peace Prize. Meanwhile he described Jonas Savimbi, who everybody else thought of as a terrorist, as Angola's Abraham Lincoln. Oops. And speaking of our national heroes, what about our radical forebears in the American Revolution who burned the homes of British loyalists? Were they terrorists?

2. Wiping out terrorists is sometimes unhelpful. Even if we could agree on what constitutes terrorism, it's often not obvious what we should do about it. Pakistan has done more than Iraq to support terrorism (in Kashmir), but instead of invading Pakistan, Mr. Bush has quite sensibly sent aid— for bolstering President Pervez Musharraf is the best hope for ending the violence. Circumstances vary, so sometimes we kill those engaged in terrorism, and sometimes we invite them for state visits.

The New York Times, Dec 27, 2002, pA21(N), pA21(L), col 1 (16 col in).
"A Toast to Moral Clarity; Were American Revolutionaries Terrorists?" by Nicholas D.
Kristof. © 2002 The New York Times Company.

3. In crude military terms, terrorism often works. New methods of killing people initially provoke outrage but eventually are often accepted. Henry V used longbows at Agincourt, outraging the French. British redcoats marching in neat columns were appalled by sneaky Yankees hiding behind trees. After Guernica, aerial bombing was condemned as barbaric, and in World War II the West condemned Germany's V-1 and V-2 missiles as terror weapons.

Likewise, in pessimistic moments I fear that Al Qaeda-style terrorism could become another terrible "advance" in military history. Other radical groups are no doubt enormously impressed that for only about $400,000, Al Qaeda inflicted hundreds of billions of dollars' damage on the United States. Vietcong military theorists predicted something like Qaeda-style urban guerrilla warfare, and there's a risk that it is what the future looks like.

All these problems reflect what the British scholar Adam Roberts refers to as "genuine doubts" about the term terrorism. The Reuters news service normally refuses to describe people as terrorists—outraging those all over the globe who are sure that's what their enemies are.

The objections leave moral clarity somewhat tattered. But ultimately terror's potential for becoming the methodology of every desperate organization makes it doubly important that we do all we can to delegitimize it—which is why I ultimately come down strongly in favor of President Bush's campaign for moral clarity. At a Harvard conference early this year, one of the few ideas to combat terrorism that seemed vaguely practical was this notion of mobilizing public opinion worldwide to stigmatize terrorism.

Ideally, any private group should know that if it kills civilians, it will become a pariah and discredit its own cause. The next Savimbi, Begin or Arafat should know that violence against civilians will not propel him into a presidential mansion, but into infamy.

Perhaps it is hopelessly naive to seek to make terrorism a universal taboo; perhaps a nuanced moral clarity is a contradiction in terms. Yet there is a precedent: After World War I, leading countries delegitimized the use of poison gas. Attacking attitudes isn't as dramatic as blowing up terror training camps, but ultimately could be more effective. Even an incomplete and inconsistent campaign against terror may foster enough public revulsion that frustrated Basques, Tamils, Palestinians or Americans will think twice before they seek redress with bombs.

So at this time of year, historically an opportunity for ethical reflection, it's time to raise a toast to moral clarity, however scarred it may often be by nebulousness, inconsistency and even hypocrisy, as still preferable to moral opacity.

4

Understanding Religious Terrorism

The War on Terrorism: Why It Really Will Be a Long One

Caryle Murphy

The war now being fought by U.S. military forces in Iraq means that Saddam Hussein's murderous reign is finished. And the recent capture of several senior Al Qaeda operatives gives hope that the terrorist network's lifespan has been considerably shortened. But these developments do not mean that the U.S. war on terrorism will soon be over.

Tactical initiatives, like routing the Taliban in Afghanistan and hunting down Al Qaeda, are insufficient to win that war and ensure our long-term safety in what is a very small world these days. What is still missing—and expected of a superpower—is a sophisticated long-term strategy, supported by patience and perseverance, for combating the roots of the religious terrorism that struck our country with such fury on Sept. 11, 2001.

For this, we need to understand the reasons for the combustible environment in today's Middle East. This is not excusing terrorism, nor is it a sign of weakness. On the contrary, such understanding fortifies us. Knowledge is power.

During five years as a correspondent in the Middle East, I learned that most Arab Muslims do not hate us, though they do hate some of our foreign policies. They certainly do not hate us for our freedoms. This statement tells us very little that is useful in forming U.S. policy or U.S. behavior abroad. Evildoers do indeed exist. But there are social, cultural, political and religious influences that created the conditions that gave rise to groups like Al Qaeda.

America, April 28, 2003, v1,88, i15, p8.
"Understanding Religious Terrorism" by Caryle Murphy. Full Text: © 2003 All rights reserved. http://americamagazine.org

The situation in the Middle East today is the result of the convergence of three major historical forces that have been unfolding for decades: first, Islam's reawakening as it comes to terms with modernity; second, the failure of the international community, in particular the United States, to resolve the long-running Israeli-Palestinian conflict, now more than a half-century old; and third, the lack of political liberties and the authoritarianism of Arab governments that has reduced Arab political life and discourse to an infantile level.

Most perplexing perhaps for Americans is the revival of Islam, which is unfolding on four distinct but complementary levels. In the daily lives of ordinary Muslims, these levels intersect and overlap. But when examined separately, they illuminate why Islam, a faith grounded in the same monotheistic tradition as Judaism and Christianity, is passing through a historic crucible.

The first level is pious Islam, by which I mean the increased personal religious devotion seen in millions of Muslims in recent decades. Whether it be stricter observance of fasting during Ramadan, wearing the veil, attending weekly study groups on the Koran or being more conscientious about saying prayers five times a day, this growing personal piety is evident in every Arab country.

The second level, political Islam, is the one that draws the headlines. But political Islam spans a wide spectrum. At one end are Islamists with a messianic mission to convert the world to their militant version of Islam. They use violence to that end. The prime example is Al Qaeda. At the other end of the spectrum are peaceful political activists, with a more tolerant brand of Islam, who reject violence. We can expect that these opposition activists will continue to use Islam as a vehicle for their activities for some years to come. And we cannot write off all of them as religious fanatics.

The third level of Islam's reawakening is cultural Islam. Many Muslims feel threatened by the powerful penetration of their societies and cultures by Western, and in particular American, culture—something that has been accelerated by globalization. In response they are returning to their roots, in other words, to Islam. This faith permeates Arab cultural life in a way that no religion, not even Christianity, penetrates Western culture.

This return to roots, or cultural Islam, is expressed in a variety of ways, some more evident than others. Some young Muslims, for example, reject Western music and films. Others are making an effort to articulate in an Islamic way, or by means of an Islamic vocabulary, values that they have come to identify—rightly or wrongly—as "Western" values: ideas like democracy, individualism, human rights and feminism. They are seeking to blend these values with their own Islamic cultural background and to express them in a way that makes sense within their Islamic world-view.

Cultural Islam is constantly in conflict with the allure of American culture. So while thousands of young Arabs love Jennifer Lopez, watch "Dallas" and rent Tom Cruise movies, others shun them. And even within the same person, there are often two colliding impulses. One says, I want to be just like those Americans. The other says, it is humiliating to imitate Americans, whose secular culture is corroding my Islamic culture.

The last manifestation of Islam's reawakening, which I call new thinking in Islam, is playing out on the theological level. Often overlooked, it is likely in the long run to be the most revolutionary aspect of this revival. Right now, more Muslims around the world are re-examining their theological heritage than at any other time in Islam's 1,300-year history. For centuries, religious scholars with years of training in Islam's sacred texts were looked to for authoritative interpretations of those texts. Now, to an unprecedented degree, ordinary Muslims are claiming the right to examine and reinterpret those texts themselves.

Essentially, Muslims are wrestling with what one young American Muslim scholar called the "interpretive imperative" to make their religion more relevant to modern times. In the process, they are grappling with big questions: What is the relationship between religious knowledge and secular knowledge? How does religious knowledge differ from religion itself? How should Islamic law, or shariah, be applied to contemporary moral and political questions? Who is to judge apostasy in a world where freedom of religious conscience is widely regarded as a basic human right? What is the relationship between political authority and God's sovereignty? And, perhaps most importantly, the key question: What is Islam's role in the public life of a modern Muslim society?

We Americans settled a similar question more than 200 years ago. Despite the lawsuits that arise every holiday season as some object to creches or menorahs in front of city hall, we enjoy a very solid national consensus about the role of religion in our country's public life. This is not so in many Muslim countries, where there has always been a close relationship between religion and politics. The Egyptian Constitution, for example, states that Islam is the official religion of the state. As a result, predominantly Muslim countries do not see the "American solution" as appropriate for them.

Islam, which has no Vatican, has always been a pluralistic faith of many interpretations. The current theological introspection is invigorating that pluralism, and all over the world thousands of competing voices are each saying, "I have the true Islam," or "This is the way Islam should be lived."

Unfortunately, at this particular moment in the Middle East, the more orthodox, more conservative and sometimes more radical voices—often espousing a literalist reading of Scripture—have the upper hand. When societies feel defensive, humiliated and beleaguered—as those in that region of the world do now—they are not at their most creative. At such times, hard-liners usually prevail. The exact opposite situation is evident in Muslim communities in the United States and Europe, where the moderate voices are the dominant ones.

It is frightening that some in the United States are taking a simplistic view of this internal struggle within Islam, equating the faith itself with its most radical, violent and anti-Western adherents. These political commentators and Christian leaders are promoting the view that Islam is at war with America, when the reality is that only a faction of radical Islamists is at war with us. In today's world of instant-messaging, insensitive remarks about Islam by people like Franklin Graham, Pat Robertson and Jerry Falwell are transmitted around the world in hours, where they fuel the growing belief that the predominantly Judeo-Christian nation of America is on a "crusade" against Islam. In such an inflamed atmosphere, remarks like these dissipate the goodwill sown by the efforts of Pope John Paul II to promote peace and Catholic-Muslim dialogue.

To win the war on terrorism, the United States must turn around the Middle Eastern environment and help moderate Muslims find their voices. But this will not be done on a dime. It is a long-range project that requires changes in U.S. policies—first of all regarding the Israeli-Palestinian conflict, which has bred such resentment and anger toward our country. President George W. Bush's recent presentation of a "road map" to resolve this conflict is a long overdue step in the right direction. But is it genuine? Will it lead to a vigorous, engaged and sustained U.S.-led international campaign to follow the road map to its destination? Or was it just a public relations exercise to pre-empt antiwar sentiment on the eve of the U.S. war against Iraq? Everyone knows what is needed to resolve this conflict in a fair and just way to both sides. The ingredients have been around for a long time. What is missing is the will and determination to implement them.

Second, the United States must confront the political frustration and economic disappointments caused by authoritarian Arab governments. It should consistently and publicly criticize human rights abuses by Middle Eastern governments, including Israel, help improve Arab education systems and encourage political liberalization.

If the United States is sincere about promoting democracy in the Arab world, it has to be patient. People accustomed to authoritarianism do not learn new ways of thinking about politics in a year. It also must realize that this process may sometimes be messy, and that elections may bring to power leaders or parties with Islamist agendas. We should be ready to distinguish between such parties—Islamists are not all the same—and judge them by their actions. With their sizeable constituencies, Islamists will likely be part of the solution of moving toward more democratic societies.

The United States also must set a good example by preserving the legal and civil rights that have made our country a beacon of freedom around the world. Lamentably, those liberties are being eroded in the name of the war on terrorism, damaging our moral authority to censure abuses in other countries.

Transforming the Middle East environment should involve not just our government, but all Americans, who have shown that when asked to contribute to their national security, they can muster a multitude of resources. Businessmen, tourism officials, university professors, scientists, political consultants and not least theologians all need to be recruited to initiate dialogue with their counterparts. The pity is that right now such contacts are diminishing.

The U.S. war in Iraq will certainly mark a historic crossroads in Arab-U.S. relations. Whether those relations improve depends not only on how the United States manages post-Hussein Iraq but also on how it addresses the roots of terrorism. Terrorists are a minority, but they win public sympathy because the United States acts arrogantly and is inconsistent in its support for democracy and short-sighted in letting the Israeli–Palestinian conflict fester.

If the United States moves strategically to transform the Middle East environment, its efforts will be well received. I know this from the many young Muslims I met there who want to be a successful part of the global community. They are moderate in religion and tolerant of other faiths. They are eager for new thinking in Islam that is compatible with democracy and modernity and that gives them a sense of restored dignity. They know deep down that a closed, cramped version of their faith will not allow Islam to maintain its vibrancy as a spiritual force. These Muslims have one eye on their computer icons and another on their minarets as they search for a moderate and modern middle way in the Middle East. All we have to do is help them find it.

Caryle Murphy, former Cairo bureau chief for The Washington Post, *is the author of* Passion for Islam.

5

Chosinness and the Theology of Terror

Dr. E. Scott Ryan presents a new word, Chosinness, to describe a new and old meta-physic that justifies criminality. He defines Chosinness as a sinful choice of choosing one God as one's God, only, to the detriment of others. Metaphysical analysis is ap-plied to criminology in indicating how a metastasis of universal spiritual chosenness can develop into a criminal quasi-religious metaphysic of Chosinness. Although this crimi-nological metaphysic of terrorism is evident in some Islamic terrorists, it is not confined to any one religion or belief system. Dr. Ryan cautions all of us as to the dangers in-herent in any Chosinness, in our needing to know how to counter this criminal meta-physical metastasis at its source in educating ourselves, as well as others, in new and old ways of thinking and believing.

In looking back to September 11th, we can look forward and back with a new word lot a very new and very old Theology of Terror. Many religious and secular words have been used, but one new religious–secular word de-fines it best. That word is Chosinness, defined by me as a sinful choice wherein one God becomes one's God, only, to the detriment of others. That new word of Chosinness represents a metastasis of the old word of Chosenness, with the new meaning of a diseased distortion of the monotheistic concept of Chosen-ness into a "chosin" Theology of Crime contortion that sanctifies terrorism with theology.

Journal of Instructional Psychology, Sept 2003, v30, i3, p237(3).
"Chosinness and the Theology of Terror" by E. Scott Ryan. © 2003 George Uhlig Publisher.

Prior to September 11th, our monotheistic religions referred to an anti-God concept of evil; and since September 11th, there's been a new secular and religious adherence to an old intrinsic notion of evil . . . in particular, a pro–God proclaiming evil that evokes a God of Terror.

In any war, military intelligence is necessary; and in this Theology of Crime War, it involves the militant metaphysics of evil that our prior intelligence failed to protect us from. Those religious leaders who taught us that evil is a mystery we can't understand have failed us, just as those secular academics who taught us that evil is an unreal religious fantasy have failed us.

The one lesson we've all learned from September 11th is that "never again" should such failures prevail. Nevertheless, we still encounter failed religious and political homilies that fail our need for counter-intelligence and counter-terrorism. Immediately after September 11, we announced to one billion Muslims that we were not an enemy of Islam; and within a year, we broadcasted Jerry Falwell's religious defamation of the Prophet, Muhammad, as a "demonic inspired pedophile." This Jerry meandering Falwellian Chosinness turns our need for a "never again" counter defense into an "ever again" offensive religious encounter that generates more hatred and conflict.

I recall the prayerful invocation of "deliver us from evil," in calling for deliverance from the religious evil of falling into the well of a Falwellian Chosinness . . . in creating the most religious enmity for us at the worst time in our history.

It's been said that war is too important to be left to the generals, and politics is too important to be left to the politicians; and it should also be said that religion is too important to be left to the likes of Jerry "Immoral Minority" Falwell.

We do need to pray for deliverance from evil, but in so doing, we also need to think about evil. The problem with countering evil is that our religious prohibitions against committing it, and our secular prohibitions against discussing it, have left us bereft of any analytic foundation with which we can encounter it so as to counter it. The unfortunate consequence is that in attempting, but failing, to prohibit evil thoughts, we've succeeded in prohibiting attempts to really think about evil . . . in prohibiting any thoughts about evil in prohibiting evil thoughts.

September 11 made us face our failures in facing up to the necessity of better counterintelligence for the purpose of better counter-terrorism. After September 11, no one could escape the realization that evil is all too real, and that our Theology of Crime War is all too religious.

I use the word "evil" in its most literal sense from the inverted spelling of "live." This terrorist inversion of life, in the literal taking of thousands of lives, can best be understood as the criminal metaphysic of Chosinness. Evil is an appropriate secular and religious word, for evil doers have done what no others have done before in bringing the ultimate evil terror of a Theology of Crime Chosinness to our shores. That criminal belief system of Chosinness must be encountered in order for counter-terrorism to succeed at the same level that the Theology of Crime terror proceeds from.

The best defense is an offense aimed at the complex points of origin of our enemy . . . Chosinness. Offensive religious descriptions of the Falwellian ilk are not only invidiously simplistic, but they are insidiously dangerous in making us more simple targets for the more simple minded. Simplistic axis of evil political responses escape the complex reality and meaning of evil in its varying commissions of wrong and omissions of right. A crusading simplicity will inevitably fail us, but it may well succeed in further endangering and isolating us.

Evil is a real religious notion and the real axis of evil revolves around religious inspired and politically implemented notions of Chosinness . . . in choosing one God as one's God for one's group, only, at the expense of others!

Enemies naturally regard each other as evil, but even if one's enemy is truly evil that natural good versus evil dichotomy obscures the not so natural nature of evil. Human nature is not evil, as Calvin taught, but one's nature becomes evil the more Chosin one is taught to become. There's often a reciprocal Chosinness of Terror wherein a metaphysical oneness is chosen by one group for themselves to the detriment of another, who then respond with their own Chosinness of Terror.

Simplistic religious assumptions about more of God and simplistic secular assumptions about less of God have proclaimed more wrong answers in the name of both pro-God and anti-God perspectives than right questions. The right questions are those that ask all of us for new perspectives with which we can name our religious God or secular Good, so as to break the "chosin" cycle of terror . . . for once and for all.

In contrast to the pre-September 11th criminal profile of a terrorist with nothing to lose, the Theology of Crime Terrorists had much to lose in the here and now . . . but even more to gain in the hereafter. At least one of them, in addition to being quite mature and well situated, pursued advanced studies at Germany's premier institute of engineering. In that respect, he reminded me of Nazi mass murderers, such as Josef Goebbels, Ph.D. and the Angel of Death, Josef Mengele, M.D., Ph.D. I include their academic and scientific credentials to illustrate that mass murder, high intelligence and elite education can coexist quite easily.

The Chosinness of the Theology of Crime terrorism is new for most Americans; but it's not new for Israelis, in being victimized by this "chosin" criminal belief rationality emanating from some in the Arab Muslim world, as well as some in their own Jewish world, to include the Chosin People who assassinated the political leader of the Chosen People, Prime Minister Yitzhah Rabin. It is not new in Northern Ireland, in not only so-called militant Catholic and Protestant bombers, but also in religious parades wherein one group celebrates victory by denigrating another with the refrain that "God is with us but not with you." It's not new for Armenian Christians, over a million of whom were massacred by Muslim Turks; just as it's not new for Bosnian Muslims in being ethnically cleansed by some Chosin among the so-called Christian Serbs, who described themselves as Chosen in defending Christianity against Islam. Just as the highly educated Arab terrorist reminds me of highly educated Nazi terrorists, and just as the assassins of Yitzhak Rabin evoke highly educated Judeo-Nazi terrorism, the Chosin terrorists who ethnically cleansed Bosnian Muslims had their own well educated political leader in Radovan Karadzic, M.D.

Our greatest enemy is not a remnant of godless Communism, or Nazism, but a terrorist who believes that God is on his or her side. This enemy attacks with a Chosin metaphysic that is a metastasis of universal Chosenness, defined as a universal spiritual choice wherein God is chosen by and for all men and women without any invidious distinction. Chosinness turns the choice of one God into a choice of one God as one's God, only . . . in turning one God for all into one's God against all others. That is the root cause of the Chosin metaphysic that drives the Theology of Crime; and whenever and wherever it transcends itself to others, it descends upon them with its terror. It can descend upon anyone from within a plane, a militant group, an oppressive state, a denigrating creed, a racist nationalism or an international cause . . . in the name of God or a Godlike substitute.

Is there something we can do to counter this etiology of terror now and in the future? Yes, but it requires something other than one group telling itself how terrible another group can be. It requires every group telling itself how terrible any Chosinness can be, to include its own; and it requires defenders of the faith in Chosenness, for all, fighting those defenders of a faith in Chosinness for themselves to the detriment of others. Those defenders must be spiritual firefighters who rush to the twin towers of religiocentricity and ethnocentricity to put out any cinders of Chosinness before they spread. In so doing, Muslims need to preach to Muslims, as to Jews to Jews and Christians to Christians rather than one group preaching at another. Secular humanists need to be reminded that while terrible people have always brought terror in the name of God, there is no God of Terror. Our politicians have to be cautioned that when they entangle America in group conflicts, most particularly religious conflicts, their political understanding must go beyond standing for what's right for one side to standing for what's right for all sides.

We cannot fight terror from without, without fighting it from within. We cannot be terrorized by fear, nor terrorize in fear. The right question as to how to counter the terror of self-serving Chosinness requires the right answer within ourselves and with others. That answer requires more spiritual warriors to help fight against the God-awful metastasis of a terrorist's God, without allowing a God of Terror to win within ourselves. The spiritual war strategy must be that of convincing the next generation that God is with us, but God is not with us if we believe God is with us only. Anyone or any group who falsely teach that they own God to the detriment of others must be taught that God has disowned them.

Dr. E. Scott Ryan. Ph.D., former Woodrow Wilson and Visiting Fellow at the U.S. Dept. of Justice, is author of The Theology of Crime, *President and CEO of the International Institute of Forensic Education, and Co-Chair of the American College of Forensic Examiners Task Force on Terrorism.*

6

Controversial Customers; Financing Terrorism

THE PLAINTIFFS' TARGET.

A Middle Eastern bank is sued in America for supporting terrorism.

IN THEORY, the world is united in fighting the financing of terrorism. In practice, the issue presents grave problems to both those attempting to prosecute it and those accused of participating in it. Just how grave is illustrated in lawsuits filed in America against Arab Bank, of Jordan, one of the largest and most geographically dispersed institutions in the Arab world. The plaintiffs accuse the bank of contributing to terrorism and murder by providing financial services to Hamas, an organisation regarded as unquestionably terrorist by America's government and others, but viewed favourably in much of the Muslim world, as well as to several smaller groups.

The most recent suit, filed on December 21st in New York's federal court, alleges that Arab Bank served "as the 'paymasters' to the families of terrorists who carried out suicide bombings" (thus providing a financial incentive for such attacks) and provided critical banking services to charitable organisations fronting for Hamas. The suit, on behalf of 700 plaintiffs, mostly from Israel, but also from 11 other countries, follows two others, the more important of which was filed last July and now includes more than 150 American plaintiffs. In all three cases the plaintiffs are seeking unspecified damages.

Arab Bank will not respond officially for several weeks. Meanwhile, through its American lawyer, Kevin Walsh of Winston & Strawn, it unequivocally denies any involvement with terrorism finance. It says that it adheres to all lists, including those prepared by American authorities, for excluding terrorism-related clients and applies know-your-customer rules to

The Economist (US), Jan 8, 2005, v374, i8408, p68US.
"Controversial Customers; Financing Terrorism." © 2005 Economist Newspaper Ltd.
Reprinted with permission.

block people with terrorist connections, including the families of suicide bombers.

This contention will be at the heart of a bitter fight over facts. Gary Osen, lead attorney in the first of the three cases, describes the suit as alleging that Arab Bank administered an elaborate "death and dismemberment plan" requiring claimants to submit certificates of martyrdom and prove they were on special lists arranged by the bank and a Saudi-based group that provided funding. Arab Bank then distributed the money through its branches in the Gaza strip and the West Bank. The involvement of Arab Bank with families of Hamas suicide bombers, adds Lee Wolosky, a lawyer on the latest case, was blatant: "There are no secrets here, everything was transparent."

The legal technicalities will draw as much interest as the arguments over fact. One question is the venue. None of the attacks took place in America and most of the participants are not American. In the past, such cases would have been moved to a more germane jurisdiction, such as Israel or Jordan. Indeed, Arab Bank's first move was to ask the court for the case to be dismissed or transferred to Amman, the Jordanian capital.

Arguments of two types were put forward for proceeding in America. Both have been heard with increasing sympathy by American courts. The first mattered most to American plaintiffs: Arab Bank has operations in New York. This office, according to the suits, played a crucial role in the financial transactions at issue. According to the July complaint, money for Hamas was raised in Saudi Arabia and then converted from riyals to dollars and shekels in Arab Bank's Madison Avenue office before being wired back to the Middle East. If true, this would violate the Anti Terrorism Act of 1990, which has taken on new prominence since September 11th 2001.

For foreign plaintiffs, America has also become more open to civil litigation under the Alien Tort Claims Act, passed in 1789, which allows them to bring cases in American courts under the "law of nations" or treaties. For two centuries it was largely ignored before being revived, primarily by human-rights activists in suits against multinational firms. Last summer, the Supreme Court left open the possibility that American courts could hear cases based on violations of universal international norms, which it did not define. The plaintiffs argue that Arab Bank has contributed to the violating of such norms by assisting Hamas in perpetuating genocide.

UNWELCOME AND UNSEEN

Whatever the results of these cases, they will have large repercussions for international banking. Many banks with global networks inevitably come into contact with clients in one country that may be considered abhorrent in another. It is quite possible that these contacts are made inadvertently. Citigroup recently sold a minority stake in a bank in Saudi Arabia after allegations of links between banks there and an account financing, among others, the Saudi Committee for the Support of the Intifada al-Quds, the fund for the families of suicide bombers that Arab Bank is alleged to have assisted (but denies having as a client). To avoid such trouble, some banks may decide that they are better off not operating in some parts of the world.

Naturally, the outcome of the case will have political as well as commercial implications. Should Arab Bank, most of whose assets are outside America, be held liable in an American court, questions may arise about whether plaintiffs could enforce the verdict in other countries. The lawsuits could also put America's government in an unenviable position, despite its condemnation of Hamas. Jordan is, after all, an important American ally, and building up its economy, which would inevitably be hurt by a setback for Arab Bank, is an aim of American foreign policy. In more than one sense, the trials in these cases have not yet begun.

II

INTERNATIONAL TERRORISM

Middle Eastern terrorist groups have been dominating the international stage for decades with al Qaeda now monopolizing the spotlight. International terrorism has become synonymous with Jihadist warfare, taking attention from other forms of international terrorism such as nationalistic, ideological, and ethnic terrorism.

7

The Global Threat

It Can Happen Anywhere; The Killers of the Global Jihad Have Only One Way of Showing They're Alive and Active: More Carnage

Michael Hirsh, Mark Hosenball, and Kevin Peraino

Jitendra Patel, a 40-year-old software developer from London, was enjoying an "absolutely brilliant" time last week with his family in Sharm al-Sheikh, a posh beach resort on the Red Sea. Patel's 7-year-old daughter, Manisha, had just finished school in the United Kingdom, and Patel needed a break, too. He had been one of those on the London Underground on July 7, making his way to work at Merrill Lynch, when the first group of bombers hit. Like thousands of other passengers, the "cheesed off" Patel had been forced to evacuate and take to the streets.

But late Friday night Patel learned just how small the world has become. Shortly after he returned to his room at the five-star Movenpick Hotel on Sharm al-Sheikh's main boulevard, his wife, Kashmira, glimpsed a split-second flash of light through the window. Then she heard a roar. The bone-jarring force of the explosion knocked loose the doorknob of the Patels' room. Across the street they saw that a car bomb had sheared away the face of the Ghazala Gardens Hotel, turning its lobby into a pile of rubble. At least 88 people died in that and two other coordinated blasts that night. Patel, who was back at the Movenpick pool sunning himself the next day, seems resigned to the new facts of global terror in the 21st century: "We can't keep running away. It's life." Kashmira Patel, on the other hand, has nothing like her husband's aplomb. "I'm frightened for everyone," she says. "It can happen to anyone, anywhere."

That seems to be the message that this latest wave of terrorists badly want to drive home. No one is safe. While no evidence connects the suicide bombers on the London transit system with the Sharm al-Sheikh car-bomb attacks, both were coordinated, fairly sophisticated plots. And each succeeded

Newsweek, August 1, 2005, p36
"The Global Threat" by Michael Hirsh, Mark Hosenball, and Kevin Peraino. © 2005 Newsweek, Inc.

in two of the most terror-vigilant nations in the world: Britain and Egypt. Both countries have built effective counterterrorism operations for decades— but for both, the July attacks were their deadliest ever. One of the London bombers, Mohammed Sidique Khan, had even gotten into Israel—perhaps the most security-conscious state in the world—on his British passport in February 2003 with a group of other ethnic Pakistani Brits, Israeli officials said. (Two months later a Pakistani Brit blew himself up at a Tel Aviv cafe, killing three people.)

The style of the London and Sharm al-Sheikh attacks bore some similarities, too. In Sharm, three bombs went off simultaneously at 1:15 a.m. Saturday, more than two miles apart. In London on July 7, four bombers hit three subway trains and a bus at almost exactly the same moment as well. Last Thursday, four more London bombers who were believed to be part of the same terror network tried again but the bombs fizzled. The quick second strike was in itself unusual: Qaeda-related groups typically launch one big attack, then lie low for a while. British investigators now believe the explosives used in last Thursday's dud bombs were likely from the same batch as the explosives used in the July 7 bombings, which also matched a cache of explosives left in a car by the suspects at the Luton railway station north of London.

Why did the second round of bombs fail to detonate? According to a U.S. official, early indications are that the people who put them together had to use "improvised detonators" because better ones were seized by police from the car left at Luton, and the homemade explosives had degraded. The four suspects who attempted last week's London bombings were still at large late last week. Security forces chased down another suspect and shot him dead on the subway in front of terrified passengers. But then, a day later, embarrassed authorities announced the dead man, Jean Charles de Menezes, 27, was a Brazilian who was not connected to the July 21 terrorist attacks at all.

Another disturbing sign of a broad-based resurgence of Qaeda-style terrorism is the roster of victims. As in Iraq, it's not just the infidels of the West who are being targeted, but any Muslims who ally themselves with the United States and other Western powers or work for their companies. After the London bombings, some Muslim clerics began speaking out more forthrightly against extremism. And at a conference earlier this month in Jordan, a group of Sunni clerics declared an end to their centuries-old internecine war with Shiites. But bombers like those in Sharm al-Sheikh may be trying to terrorize the Muslim community into silence again. At least two of the bombs were likely aimed at tourists, at the Ghazala Gardens and at a popular boardwalk. But the majority of victims were Egyptian, and one of the targets hit Friday night was a cafe in the Old Market, where many Egyptian workers congregate. Also last week, two bombs went off in the streets of Beirut, Lebanon, only hours after a visit by U.S. Secretary of State Condoleezza Rice. There were no deaths, but one explosion targeted popular Monot Street, which is frequented by Arab tourists.

This harrowing message to fellow Muslims—keep away from the infidel or die—was also delivered last week by an Islamist Web site frequently used by the group led by Abu Mussab al-Zarqawi, Al Qaeda's leader in Iraq. After Algeria's envoy was kidnapped last week, the site posted a statement: "Algeria rushed to obey the crusaders by sending its envoy to Iraq . . . did you not learn from the fate of the ambassador of the Egyptian tyrant?" (Terrorists killed the Egyptian ambassador last month.) "They just want to kill to say to the world, 'We are still here and we are still strong and we can hit when-ever we want'," says Huthaifa Azzam, the son of Abdullah Azzam, the Palestinian-born organizer of the "Arab Afghans" who fought against the Russians in the 1980s and provided the core recruits of Osama bin Laden's Al Qaeda.

Investigators and analysts say it is difficult to create a profile of this latest generation of terrorists. Many appear to be young men who have spontaneously created cells in their home countries—with perhaps some outside help from a skilled "facilitator." The London bomb plotters, who authorities say could number more than two dozen, included Britons of Pakistani ethnicity, while the Madrid train bombers of March 2004 were mostly Spanish nationals of Moroccan extraction. Egyptian investigators over the weekend were unsure of the identity of the Sharm plotters, but one witness account at the Old Market said a man announced, "I have a bomb," in Egyptian Arabic shortly before it went off. A group called the Abdullah Azzam Brigades, Al Qaeda in Syria and Egypt, claimed responsibility. This was one of two extremist groups that also claimed responsibility for October bombings at two other Egyptian resorts, in Taba and Ras Shitan, which killed 34.

Whoever the terrorists are, they seem intent on driving wedges between the United States and its allies in both Iraq and in the broader war on terror, one by one. Some Brits looking for reasons for the July 7 and July 21 attacks blamed Prime Minister Tony Blair's support of the Iraq war, which is deeply unpopular in Britain. The London bombings also provoked a testy exchange between Blair and Pakistani President Pervez Musharraf, whose country has allegedly become a kind of jihadist finishing school, where some would-be terrorists seem to get operational knowledge and final instructions. "The problem is not in Pakistan; the problem is in England," Musharraf insisted to ABC News.

Many of these new native-born terror cells don't need much recruitment from abroad or training in Afghan-style camps—the old Qaeda model. When one of the July 7 bombers, Shahzad Tanweer, visited Pakistan in late 2004 and early 2005, he told his family that he was going to attend a Pakistani religious school, or madrassa, to further his religious education. But Ahmed Rashid, a Pakistani expert on extremist groups, says Tanweer and his fellow bombers were likely "fully indoctrinated on arrival" thanks to their radical connections in Britain. Adds Christine Fair of the U.S. Institute of Peace: "The Pakistani diaspora [abroad] appears to be the place where people are radicalizing. They go to Pakistan for training."

For international investigators, the only sensible approach is to work even more closely together. British and U.S. authorities appear to have established clear connections between some of the suspected perpetrators of the July 7 suicide bombings in London and a plot that was broken up early last year by British authorities—with the help of an American informant named Mohammed Junaid Babar—to bomb unspecified targets in the London area. That counterterrorism operation was code-named Operation Crevice. U.S., British and Pakistani officials also cooperated behind the scenes to capture another man who may be connected to the July 7 bombings and whose name turned up in the Operation Crevice databases, according to a senior U.S. official who declined to be identified because of the sensitivity of his work. This is Haroon Rashid Aswat, a native-born Briton of Indian or Pakistani ancestry, who may have played a critical role in this and other plots. In the late 1990s, Aswat served as a sidekick to one of London's most notorious jihadist imams, the hook-handed Egyptian-born preacher Abu Hamza al-Mazri. He was also linked to a failed effort to set up a terrorist training camp in Oregon. U.S. officials said that the names of two of the July 7 bombers, Khan and Germaine Lindsay, also turned up in Operation Crevice. An official familiar with the London investigation told NEWSWEEK late last week that Aswat has been quietly captured and will soon undergo questioning.

That may help investigators desperately trying to avert the next attack before it happens. But the broader question is how to prevent another generation of terrorists from being created. British and European investigators who evince a new get-tough approach to terror within their borders may open themselves to the same kind of accusations the Americans face: that they are targeting the innocent as well as the guilty, and thereby generating more terrorists. British police indicated on Saturday that the man they mistakenly shot on the tube was followed because he "emerged from a block of flats in the Stockwell area that were under police surveillance." The police statement added: "For somebody to lose their life in such circumstances is a tragedy and one that the Metropolitan Police Service regrets." Would that the terrorists expressed similar regrets about the deaths of innocents. Instead, "increasingly we are seeing attacks either in the West or in Iraq or in Egypt that are purely nihilistic," says Bill Durodie of Britain's Royal Military College of Science. "We are seeing terrorism that is an end in itself." And that has no end in sight.

8

The Struggle for the Soul of Islam

Mark Silverberg

Many of the sources that I review on a daily basis are translations of the Arab press that are produced by the Middle East Media Research Institute (MEMRI). In an issue last year of Sawt al-Jihad ("Voice of Jihad"), a site identified with al Qaeda, an article appeared titled "A Letter to the Wife of the Slain Pagan Paul Johnson from the Wife of One of the Martyrs." The letter celebrates the murder of the American hostage Paul Johnson in Saudi Arabia and is attributed to the wife of one of the terrorists who was subsequently killed by the Saudi Security forces.

In it, the unnamed letter-writer wrote: "I swear to God that I was extremely happy that day, for the true terrorist was killed, after having sucked the blood of our Muslim children." It continued, "The blood of your husband is the blood of a dog because he is an idolatrous infidel." (MEMRI, Special Dispatch—Saudi Arabia/Jihad & Terrorism Studies Project, August 5, 2004 No. 758)

This was followed by a *New York Times* article that stated that al Qaeda's upper ranks are being manned by lower-ranking members and more recent recruits filling the vacuum created when its leaders are killed or captured. In other words, the madrassas continue to teach the young to hate and to churn out suicide bombers. This, we cannot control. Thus, it becomes clear that for Western civilization to triumph over Islamic barbarism, fundamental changes must first occur within Islam itself.

For the first time since the Crusades, Western civilization finds itself involved in a religious war. As Shmuel Bar has noted in his probing analysis of

Midstream, March–April 2005, v51, i2, p12(2).
"The Struggle for the Soul of Islam" by Mark Silverberg. © 2005 Theodor Herzl Foundation.

modern-day Islam, a counter-terrorism strategy to fight radical Islam must begin at the religious-ideological level, not at the political or legal level. The Report of the 9/11 Commission goes far in detailing the political and legal options, but it says little of the religious/ideological ones.

The reason the Commission dodged the issue is simple. In addressing this Islamic phenomenon, the West is at a severe disadvantage. Western concepts of civil rights, along with legal, political, and cultural constraints, preclude any government intervention in the internal affairs of organized religions. As a result, our laws make it difficult to prohibit or punish inflammatory sermons of imams in mosques or to punish clerics for decrees (fatwas) justifying terrorism. They are free to spread their ideology of death from pulpits throughout America. These sermons are seen as exercises in free speech. However, because we are involved in an ideological (more so than a territorial) war, it is a dangerous mistake to skirt this issue. By doing nothing, we cede the ideological field to radical Islam in our own country. And so do the moderate leaders of Islam in America and around the world.

Even the Patriot Act deals primarily with investigative powers (such as allowing for unlimited administrative arrests, etc.) and does not deal with the prohibition of religion-based "ideological crimes" (such as the anti-Nazi and anti-racism laws that are in force in many countries including Canada and Europe). France, for example, has taken one of the hardest lines of any Western country in fighting Islamic extremism. It has expelled many Muslim preachers who foment anti-Western sentiment and violence in their sermons. However much we may dislike French foreign policy, that country has recognized that terrorist acts cannot be separated from the words that feed them.

And therein lies the problem for many Americans. A strategy designed to cope with radical Islamic ideology cannot take shape without a reinterpretation of our own Western concepts of the limits of our freedoms of religion and speech, our definitions of religious incitement, and the criminal culpability of religious leaders for the acts of their flock as a result of their spiritual influence and dangerous sermons. Such a reinterpretation impinges upon the basic principles of Western civilization and Western laws. But where the alternative is allowing radical Islam to grow in our midst, I suspect that redefining the limits of our religious and free speech laws may be the lesser of the two evils.

For all these reasons, it is difficult for us to prevent the conversion of young Muslims in the West to the ideas of radical Islam emanating from the safe houses of the Middle East unless radical Islam itself is attacked as a perverted ideology. Thus, the goal of the West cannot be to fight this war defensively or even offensively, and even the democratization of the Middle East (although it may be part of the ultimate solution—if it is doable). Rather, the goal must include a "religious-ideological dimension" to this war—active pressure for religious reform in the Muslim world and pressure on the orthodox Islamic establishment in the West and the Middle East not only to disengage itself clearly from any justification of violence, but also to pit itself against the radical camp in a clear demarcation of boundaries.

Such disengagement, unfortunately, cannot be accomplished by non-Muslims. It can only be achieved by clear and binding legal decrees (fatwas) from moderate, respected Muslim religious authorities who contradict the axioms of the radicals' worldview and virtually excommunicate these radicals. In essence, the radical narrative (which promises "paradise" to those who perpetrate acts of terrorism against infidels) must be met by an equally legitimate religious force that guarantees damnation for the same acts.

Some elements of the kinds of decrees (fatwas) necessary could include:

- a call for a renewal of ijtihad (understanding) as the basis to reform Islamic dogmas and to relegate old dogmas to historic contexts;

- that there exists no state of jihad between Islam and the rest of the world (hence, jihad is not a personal duty);

- that the violation of the physical safety of a non-Muslim in a Muslim country is prohibited (haram) by the Qur'an;

- that suicide bombings are clear acts of suicide, and therefore, their perpetrators are condemned to eternal damnation;

- that moral or financial support of these acts of terrorism is prohibited (haram);

- that any legal ruling that claims jihad is a duty derived from the roots of Islam is a falsification of the roots of Islam, and therefore, those who make such statements have performed acts of heresy.

Only by discrediting radical Islam throughout the Muslim world can the radical elements of al Qaeda (and its terror franchisees) be exorcised and a clash of our two civilizations be averted.

But there is a problem internal to Islam that is complicating this effort. Islamic law demands "unity of faith" within the Islamic world. This plays into the hands of the radicals. For the sake of unity, moderates withhold their dissent, believing that the alternative to "spiritual unity" is "spiritual chaos." In effect, they have conceded the struggle and left the playing field to the radicals.

The internal struggle between orthodox Islam and radical Islam must be based on an in-depth understanding of the religious sources for justification of Islamic terrorism and a plan for the creation of a legitimate moderate counterbalance to the radical narrative in Islam. Such an alternative narrative should have a sound base in Islamic teachings, and its proponents should be Islamic scholars and leaders with wide legitimacy and accepted credentials.

The war on Islamic terrorism cannot be won unless Islam itself is modernized and moderated in the same way that Christian and Jewish scholars have (over the centuries) moderated the more strident aspects of their scriptures and promoted those verses that spoke of the brotherhood of man, tolerance, and understanding.

We may kill millions of Islamic extremists throughout the world, but unless we recognize that we are engaged in an ideological war, and unless the radical ideology of Islam is discredited by its own moderate Islamic scholars, our political and legal remedies will not be able to stem the tide of this Islamic scourge.

Islam awaits its Reformation. And so does the world.

MARK SILVERBERG is an attorney and executive director of the Jewish Federation of Northeastern Pennsylvania in Scranton, PA. He has published numerous articles on American foreign policy in the Middle East and on global terrorism. His articles have been archived under his name on the Internet.

9

Who Are the Suicide Bombers?

Owais Tohid

KARACHI, PAKISTAN—In four years, 28-year-old Gul Hasan went from laying bricks to recruiting suicide bombers. An antiterrorism court convicted Mr. Hasan this month of planning suicide attacks on Shiite mosques in Karachi that killed dozens of worshipers. Now he faces the gallows.

How people like Hasan get involved with militant Islam, and what they do to recruit others, are questions of increasing urgency in Pakistan, which has seen a spate of suicide bombings in recent weeks.

The attacks were carried out by splinter groups formed in the wake of a Pakistani crackdown on militant Islamic organizations after Sept. 11, 2001. Smaller and more isolated than their parent organizations, these splinter groups receive financial backing from Al Qaeda and draw their recruits from the ranks of the poor and enraged, say Pakistani investigators.

"This is a new breed [of militants], as suicide bombings are a post 9/11 phenomenon here," says Fateh Mohammad Burfat, head of the Criminology Department at the University of Karachi. The bombers are "unemployed, illiterate, and belong to poor social strata. [They also] perceive the US military actions in Iraq and Afghanistan as hostile acts against the Muslim world. . . . By suicide attacks, they get a sense of victory in the world and hereafter."

Hasan entered the world of militant Islam when his brother, a member of the splinter group Lashkar-e Jhangvi, was arrested. Over time, Hasan went from being a simple carrier of weapons to a dangerous militant leader in Karachi responsible for recruiting and transporting suicide bombers, say police officials.

The Christian Science Monitor (*www.csmonitor.com*), June 17, 2005, p07.

RISING THROUGH THE RANKS

The splinter groups "provide the new entrants with poisonous extremist literature to brainwash them, and then start giving them responsibilities from shifting weapons to providing refuge to wanted militants," says Gul Hameed Samoo, a Karachi police official. "One rises through the ranks after fulfilling [certain] tasks."

The leaders recruit them for different purposes, with agendas ranging from killing Shiites to liberating Muslims from "infidels." The new trend of suicide bombings is packaged as a "ticket to Paradise."

Many of the splinter groups' top leadership fought in Afghanistan and Kashmir. They are believed to have made contacts and trained with Arab militants in Afghanistan.

Police investigators describe three layers of organization behind suicide attacks. In most of the cases, the mastermind is Al Qaeda, which gets in touch through a courier with the leader of a jihadi splinter group who plans the attack. The attacker is often a "brainwashed" jihadi.

In the case of the unsuccessful suicide attack against Pakistani President Pervez Musharraf on Christmas Day 2003, police say the mastermind was Abu Faraj, an Al Qaeda operative now in custody; the planner was Amjad Farooqi; the slain chief of Lashkar-e Jhangvi; and the bomber was a local jihadi.

In a *New York Times* opinion piece on Tuesday, Peter Bergen, author of "Holy War, Inc.," and Swati Pandey argued that the Islamic terrorists behind many of the attacks against the West are well-educated—not brainwashed youth from madrassahs, or Islamic schools. In a sampling of 75 terrorists involved in attacks against Westerners, they found that 53 percent had attended college—a figure slightly higher than US averages. "[Madrassahs] are not and should not be considered a threat to the United States," the authors wrote.

In Pakistan, where many of the suicide attacks do not directly target Westerners, the Al Qaeda masterminds are often well-educated, but the planners and the bombers themselves generally are not.

"There are leaders who look out for suicide bombers and usually find the simple, unemployed religious-minded youth with the help of a cleric at a mosque or madrassah," says a police investigator.

BOMBER DROPOUTS

Hasan, the recruiter of suicide bombers, has an eighth-grade education. Mohammad Jamil, one of the two suicide bombers behind the Christmas attack on Mr. Musharraf, was a dropout who studied at a madrassah in Pakistan's Frontier Province. Neither Mohammad Ali Khatri nor Akbar Niazi, two suicide bombers who killed 40 worshipers at two Shiite mosques last year, completed high school.

Recent interrogations have shed light on how bombers are recruited and groomed. A police investigator quoted a detained sectarian militant, identified as Tehseen, as saying, "We isolate the boy who is willing to sacrifice his life. From then onwards he does not have any contact with his family or friends. We provide him religious books, and he prays all the time before [his] mission."

Police nabbed Tehseen after he was injured at the scene of an attack on a Shiite mosque in Karachi this month. He was accompanying the suicide bomber as a guard.

"In some cases, the suicide bomber gets terrified after reaching the target and flees. [The leaders] sometimes take the family hostage if the suicide bomber changes his mind," the police investigator says.

The suicide-bomber cells operate in small groups of five to seven people, never staying at one place for more than two nights, says a police investigator.

Moving in small cells is now a necessity for members of the larger splinter groups, which have been thrown into disarray by a persistent government crackdown, officials say. They add that the isolation of splinter groups, as well as their greater dependence on outside funding, may explain the adoption of the radical tactic of suicide bombing.

"They are on the run, and short of resources. But it is the most dangerous tactic and rather impossible to stop like elsewhere in the world," says Karachi police chief Tariq Jameel. "We have to create awareness and counter them by eliminating extremism from the society, which is the best antidote to terrorism. Otherwise suicide bombings can give these disarrayed splinter groups a new life."

Last month, a group of 58 religious scholars issued a fatwa, or religious edict, saying that Islam strictly forbids suicide attacks on Muslims. Further, those committing such acts at public congregations or places of worship cease to be Muslims.

"Killing of any non-Muslim citizen or foreigner visiting the country is also forbidden in Islam since they are under protection of government of Pakistan," said Mufti Munib-ur Rehman, one of those issuing the edict.

10

Europe Confronts Changing Face of Terrorism

Elaine Sciolino

One attack was deadly, the other was not. But taken together, the two terrorist strikes that hit London in July highlight a new, more ominous face of terrorism in Europe.

It transcends ethnic lines and national causes, blends ideological fervor with common criminality and is rooted to a large extent inside the target country. Shifting assumptions about the nature of the terrorist threat, it also complicates efforts to devise strategies to combat it.

Although some senior intelligence and law enforcement officials said they began to recognize the mutating threat at the time of the train bombings in Madrid in March 2004, the London bombings have reinforced the lesson that, by all accounts, the centrally controlled Al Qaeda of 9/11 is no more.

"We are seeing a terrorist threat that keeps changing," said Pierre de Bousquet, the director of France's domestic intelligence service, known as the D.S.T., in an interview in Paris. "Often the groups are not homogeneous, but a variety of blends."

"Hard-core Islamists are mixing with petty criminals," he added. "People of different backgrounds and nationalities are working together. Some are European-born or have dual nationalities that make it easier for them to travel. The networks are much less structured than we used to believe. Maybe it's the mosque that brings them together, maybe it's prison, maybe it's the

The New York Times, August 1, 2005, pA1(L).
"Europe Confronts Changing Face of Terrorism" by Elaine Sciolino. © 2005 The New York Times Company.

neighborhood. And that makes it much more difficult to identify them and uproot them."

In the case of the London attacks of July 7 that left 56 people dead, including the four bombers, three of the attackers were ethnic Pakistanis born in Britain, the fourth a British citizen and convert to Islam born in Jamaica.

The strike that followed two weeks later, in which the four bombs did not explode, was carried out by an intriguing crew that the police say included a British resident born in Somalia, an Ethiopian who apparently posed as a Somali refugee to gain legal residency in Britain and a British citizen born in Eritrea who acquaintances say was radicalized in prison. The nationality and legal status of the fourth would-be bomber has not been disclosed.

The police still say they have not found conclusive evidence linking the two attacks, although the explosives used in both cases, as well as other elements of the episodes, appear to be similar.

None of those identified so far as being involved in the two attacks are believed to have been a battle-hardened veteran of Chechnya or Iraq, and most of them are too young to have been trained in Qaeda camps in Afghanistan, which were destroyed in 2001. They may have learned their bomb-making techniques and terrorist strategies at home, investigators and intelligence officials say, although the officials caution that they do not yet know the extent of the support network behind the attacks or whether either involved a foreign mastermind.

Britain's most senior counterterrorism official himself anticipated what was happening over a year ago. In a little-noticed speech to a conference in Florence in June 2004, Peter Clarke, the counterterrorism chief of Britain's police force, pointed out "the complete change, the recalibration" that Britain was making in investigating the new threat.

The shifting nature of the threat was made apparent early last year with Operation Crevice, one of Britain's largest counterterrorism operations ever, Mr. Clarke said. Seven hundred officers thwarted what they believed was a plot to construct a large bomb intended for a site somewhere in London. In more than two dozen police raids, more than half a ton of ammonium nitrate fertilizer, which can be used in making bombs, was seized and eight ethnic Pakistani British citizens were arrested.

"Before this there was the perception that the international terrorist threat was something that came from abroad," Mr. Clarke said in the speech. "It came from the Maghreb. It came from the Middle East. It came from Chechnya. It came from Afghanistan. These individuals, however, were all British citizens."

"The parameters," he said, "have changed completely."

"If we take one or two leaders away," he added, "very quickly they are replaced and the network is reformed."

He called the homegrown trend "deeply worrying." Equally worrying, he added, was that the "key conspirator" in the plot revealed by Operation Crevice was only 22 years old, and that others were 18 and 19.

A confidential British government assessment of the emerging threat from young British Muslim radicals, prepared last year for Prime Minister Tony Blair, concludes that poverty is not an indication of radicalism, that students and young professionals from working- and middle-class backgrounds "have also become involved in extremist politics and even terrorism." Those recruits, the report warns, "may have the capability for wider and more complex proselytizing."

Extremist organizations have set up outlets on university campuses and, if banned, simply open up again under different names, said the document, whose contents were first disclosed in *The Sunday Times*. The document divides young extremists into two broad categories. The first category is "well-educated undergraduates" and those "with degrees and technical professional qualifications in engineering" or information technology. The second is "underachievers with few or no qualifications, and often a criminal background."

In particular, the report said, "Muslims are more likely than other faith groups to have no qualifications (over two-fifths have none) and to be unemployed and economically inactive, and are over-represented in deprived areas."

The idea that the terrorist threat is increasingly homegrown and transcends both ethnicity and direct links to a global Qaeda conspiracy is welcomed by Pakistan, which has been accused of not doing enough to root out the remnants of Al Qaeda. Three of the four bombers in the first London attack were of Pakistani descent and at least two had spent time in Pakistan.

"When the first bombing happened and everyone focused on Pakistan, we said, 'You may be making a mistake if you have a unifocal view,'" said Maleeha Lodhi, Pakistan's ambassador to Britain, in an interview. "It's much more mixed up than people think. What you're seeing is something very lethal and it has nothing to do with ethnicity."

"We are seeing a lot of local groups that seem to have a random pattern, no operational linkage or even inspirational linkage," she said. "Some may claim to be Al Qaeda, some not, and that is foxing everybody."

Earlier attacks reflected some of the same elements found in the London bombings. First came Casablanca, then Madrid.

In May 2003, a dozen young, poor, undereducated men, all born and reared in the same slum in Casablanca, Morocco, attacked five sites there, four apparently chosen for their Jewish connections. Forty-two people died, including the attackers.

"It was local guys thinking global," said Olivier Roy, author of the book "Globalized Islam."

"They didn't target a symbol of the Moroccan government," he added. "They inscribed their actions in a global perspective. I'm not sure the ethnic Pakistanis involved in the first London attacks have anything to do with Pakistan."

The train attacks in Madrid in March last year represented more of a blend. While most of those involved were Moroccan, some were from other countries. Some of the attackers were radicalized Muslims, others common criminals.

The most senior member of the team, and the suspected local leader of the cell, was a Tunisian who aspired to be a fashion model but became a successful real estate agent before turning radical.

The Madrid plotters included native Spaniards, who had no connection to global jihad, including a former miner who was arrested on charges that he stole and handled the explosives used in the operation and a 16-year-old nick-named "The Gypsy" who was given a six-year youth detention sentence last November after pleading guilty to transporting explosives. In searching for the mastermind of the Madrid attacks, the Spanish authorities have focused on a number of foreign-based suspects, including an Egyptian and a Syrian.

In London, investigators are trying to determine whether the cells involved in the attacks were homegrown or had any operational link to a wider network.

Investigators say that while they see the terrorism threat in Europe as more homegrown, the inspiration is increasingly Iraq. In the past several months, a number of European countries have uncovered cells of native-born men poised to travel to Iraq to fight alongside the insurgency.

In an interview published in *Le Parisien* on Friday, Interior Minister Nicolas Sarkozy of France said at least seven Frenchmen had been killed while fighting with the insurgency in Iraq.

The ever-shifting nature of the threat has made it increasingly challenging, in Britain and elsewhere, to come up with a strategy to combat it. Police and intelligence officials acknowledge that they are still too focused on threats linked to clearly identifiable ethnic radical groups, both domestic and international, and not enough on homegrown blends.

In a cover letter to the 2004 British report on counter-terrorism, Sir Andrew Turnbull, the cabinet secretary and one of Mr. Blair's closest aides, said the goal of Britain's strategy was "to prevent terrorism by tackling its underlying causes, to work together to resolve regional conflicts to support moderate Islam and reform and to diminish support for terrorists by influencing relevant social and economic issues."

But, he added, "without being clear about the nature of the problem, one can only tentatively identify possible responses in general terms."

11

Masters of Suicide Bombing: Tamil Guerrillas of Sri Lanka

Amy Waldman

nside the Kantharuban Arivuchcholai orphanage, which is set in a clearing hacked from the jungle's oppressive vegetation, sits a small painted hut, a mini-museum of sorts.

Inside it is a picture of Kantharuban, who blew himself up in 1991. There is a picture of Captain Millar, who blew himself up in 1987. There is a picture of 12 cadres of the Liberation Tigers of Tamil Eelam who swallowed cyanide capsules after capture by Indian troops in 1987.

Eleven-year-old Rajani, who calls the orphanage home, knows them all. He knows that Kantharuban, an orphan like him, asked that the home be founded. Captain Millar, Rajani said, was "the first Black Tiger," a member of the special suicide unit of the rebels, who have been fighting for a homeland for the Tamil ethnic minority in Sri Lanka for two decades.

"They go in sea and on land in black robes," he said, proud of his knowledge. "They will go and jam themselves against anything."

When Captain Millar plowed a truck full of explosives into an army camp in July 1987, 40 soldiers died, along with the captain, and a culture was born.

It has elevated the suicide attack to the ultimate commitment to the movement.

The New York Times, Jan 14, 2003, pA1(N), pA1(L), col 4, (20 col in).
"Masters of Suicide Bombing: Tamil Guerrillas of Sri Lanka" by Amy Waldman. © 2003
The New York Times Company.

The Tigers did not invent the suicide attack, but they proved the tactic to be so unnerving and effective for a vastly outmanned fighting force that their methods were studied and copied, notably in the Middle East.

"Of all the suicide-capable terrorist groups we have studied, they are the most ruthless, the most disciplined," said Rohan Gunaratna, a research fellow at the Center for the Study of Terrorism and Political Violence at the University of St. Andrews in Scotland. He said the group was responsible for more than half of the suicide attacks carried out worldwide.

In the 15 years since Captain Millar's attack—starting before the tactic was widely used in the Palestinian-Israeli conflict or by the Al Qaeda pilots who rammed passenger planes into two of the world's tallest buildings—the Liberation Tigers of Tamil Eelam became the world's foremost suicide bombers, sending out about 220 attackers in all.

Until Sept. 11, "they were the deadliest terror organization in the world," one American official said. They used men, women, children and animals; boats, trucks and cars. They mounted suicide attacks on the battlefield as well as off.

Suicide bombers killed one Sri Lankan president, wounded another and killed a former Indian prime minister. They took out government ministers, mayors and moderate Tamil leaders, decimating the country's political and intellectual leadership.

They attacked naval ships—destroying a third of the Sri Lankan Navy—and oil tankers; the airport in Colombo, the capital; the Temple of the Tooth, home to Sri Lanka's most sacred Buddhist relic; and Colombo's own World Trade Center. They killed certainly hundreds, and possibly thousands, of civilians, although civilians were never their explicit target.

Their killing innovations were studied.

Mr. Gunaratna said the attack on the American destroyer *Cole* by Al Qaeda in 2000 had been almost identical to a Tiger attack on a Sri Lankan naval ship in 1991. The head of the Sea Tigers, Soosai, who organized suicide attacks on boats, oil tankers and the like, boasted in a recent BBC interview that the *Cole* attack had been copied from the Tigers.

The Tigers evolved ever more sophisticated suicide bodysuits, and more refined surveillance. They skillfully insinuated themselves within striking distance of their targets. They professionalized, and institutionalized, suicide bombing.

Today, actions by the Black Tigers and the Sea Tigers are being held in abeyance.

The Tigers have declared and observed a cease-fire and are at the negotiating table trying to reach a political settlement with the Sri Lankan government.

For the first time in years, Tiger territory is easily accessible to the outside world. Much like the orphanage with its shrine, it has revealed itself as a place steeped in the notion of self-sacrifice.

Pictures of suicide attackers like Captain Millar are commonplace. The Tigers sometimes filmed their suicide attacks, and a store in Kilinochchi, their administrative headquarters, sells CD's with tribute songs to the Black Tigers and videodiscs of the attack on the airport.

A large billboard along the A-9 road, which runs through Tiger territory on its way north, shows women how to fully exploit their deaths. If wounded in battle, colorful graphics demonstrate, they are to play dead until enemy soldiers approach, and then blow up as many as possible—and themselves in the process.

Suicide has long been part of the Tiger culture. Tigers were given cyanide capsules and told to use them if captured. Many did.

But suicide bombing was an offensive weapon, not a defensive one. It was devised to make up for the Tamils' numerical disadvantage—their population is about one-fourth that of the majority Sinhalese—and to flummox the country's military and political leadership.

The goal, S. Thamilchelvam, the Tigers' political head, said, was "to ensure maximum damage done with minimum loss of life."

The Tigers have long claimed overt responsibility only for attacks on military sites. In their graveyard outside Kilinochchi, there are headstones without bodies for many Black Tigers and Sea Tigers.

But there are none for those whom S. Tamilarasan, a 22-year-old aide in the political wing, called "the indirect"—those involved in attacks on sites, like the Colombo airport, or leaders that were too politically sensitive to claim.

In an interview, Mr. Thamilchelvam said the Tigers had hit only military targets, but then conceded that political targets had been attacked as well.

The separation of the political and the military makes sense in the Western context, he said, but not in Sri Lanka, which has largely been governed by the Sinhalese since independence in 1948.

"In the politics of Sri Lanka the military is only an instrument of a genocidal policy, of annihilation, of trying to weaken the Tigers," he said. "You cannot find a distinction between the political hierarchy and a military soldier. Political decisions, unfortunately, in Sri Lanka become military policy or action."

For the movement, the Black Tigers acquired more than utilitarian value. Considered the most heroic of Tiger fighters, they became as well symbols of the loyalty that the movement for a Tamil state—and its leader, Vellupillai Prabhakaran—commanded.

"Every Tiger is committed to end his or her life for the goal," Mr. Thamichelvam said.

The Tigers abjure the phrase suicide bombing. Mr. Thamilchelvam cited two words in Tamil. One, "thatkolai," means to kill yourself. The other, "thatkodai," means to give yourself. That was the word the Tigers used, and preferred.

"It is a gift of the self—self-immolation, or self-gift," he said. "The person gives him or herself in full."

That commitment defined the Tiger fighter, he said. "When one enlists, there is no remuneration. The only promise is I am prepared to give everything I have, including my life. It is an oath to the nation."

Cadres applied to be Black Tigers, communicating their desire to Mr. Prabhakaran, according to Thamilini, the 30-year-old head of the female cadres. Some 30 to 40 percent of their suicide bombers, including the one who killed former Prime Minister Rajiv Gandhi of India in 1991, have been women.

A reply would come from Mr. Prabhakaran, she said. Sometimes it was an outright refusal. More often, she said, this answer came back: "There are many applicants. Do what duties are sent to you. If the necessity arises we'll call you."

Those selected to be Black Tigers underwent intense physical and psychological training and reportedly a last dinner with Mr. Prabhakaran. That was when Kanthaburan, for whom the orphanage here is named, made his request that a home be created for parentless children like him, said Puviavyasan, the Tiger who runs the orphanage.

Those selected, said Thamilini, were strong in spirit and firm in purpose. She explicitly rejected any comparison to Palestinian suicide bombers, who she suggested were often dejected in life.

"People dejected in life won't be able to go as Black Tigers," she said. "There must be a clear conception of why and for what we are fighting. A deep humanitarianism is very necessary—a love of others, for the people."

Tiger bombings have killed at minimum hundreds of civilians who were caught near the targets. The bombing of the Central Bank in 1996, done on a working day, killed at least 90 people; assassinations of political leaders have usually taken the lives of dozens of other civilians.

But Thamilini drew a distinction of intent. The Tigers' "target is not the common people, but the army," she said. "In Palestine it is quite different."

III

DOMESTIC TERRORISM

Homegrown terrorism has its roots in political extremism and violent activism. Domestic terrorists either work as a group—as do violent formations of environmental activists, anti-abortionists, and animal rights groups—or operate alone as a politically disgruntled citizen or ideologically blinded person.

12

Homegrown Terror

Homegrown Terror: A Bomb Is a Bomb. A Chemical Weapon Is a Chemical Weapon. It Won't Matter to the Victims Whether Their Attacker's Name Is Ahmed or Bill

Michael Reynolds

O N APRIL 10, 2003, A TEAM of federal agents armed with a search warrant entered a storage unit in a small Texas town and were stunned to find a homemade hydrogen cyanide device—a green metal military ammo box containing 800 grams of pure sodium cyanide and two glass vials of hydrochloric acid. The improvised weapon was the product of 62-year-old William Joseph Krar, an accomplished gunsmith, weapons dealer, and militia activist from New Hampshire who had moved his operations to east central Texas just 18 months earlier.

That same day the *New York Times's* Judith Miller reported from south of Baghdad that the U.S. Army Mobile Exploitation Team had "unearthed . . . precursors for a toxic agent . . . banned by chemical weapons treaties." That turned out not to be the case. What the army team found was fewer than two dozen barrels of organophosphate used in pesticides.

In Chicago a month earlier, Joseph Konopka, a 26-year-old anarcho-terrorist had been sentenced on one count of possession of a chemical weapon. In March 2002, Konopka, who had appropriated an abandoned Chicago Transit Authority storage room under downtown Chicago, was found and arrested in a tunnel beneath the University of Illinois at Chicago. Konopka was a fugitive from federal charges in Wisconsin, where he had hit power substations, radio transmitters, and utility facilities in a 1999 firebombing campaign that caused 28 power outages.

Bulletin of the Atomic Scientists, Nov–Dec 2004, v60, i6, p48(10).
"Homegrown Terror" by Michael Reynolds. © 2004 Educational Foundation for Nuclear Science, Inc.

An accomplished systems programmer and hacker, Konopka had assumed the online moniker of "Doc Chaos" and recruited bright teenage accomplices into a cadre he called the "Realm of Chaos." One of these accomplices was arrested with him. In a search of Konopka's subterranean outpost, authorities found nearly a pound of sodium cyanide along with substantial amounts of potassium cyanide, mercuric sulfate, and potassium chlorate.

The young man never gave a reason for why he had stockpiled the deadly chemicals, except to say they were not for "peaceful purposes." (1) He is now serving more than 21 years in federal prison for sabotage and possession of a chemical weapon.

By the time Krar pleaded guilty to one count of possession of a chemical weapon on November 11, 2003, two U.S. citizens—Krar and Konopka—were accountable for far more chemical weapons than have been found in post-war Iraq.

CHEMICAL CAPERS

Without diminishing the significance of Konopka's attacks on local infrastructure in Wisconsin, Krar's is the more disturbing case, given the size and capabilities of his arsenal, his history, his ideology, his discipline, and his expertise. Despite that, his case attracted little national media attention. There were no press conferences called by Attorney General John Ashcroft and FBI Director Robert Mueller, even though Krar presented the most demonstrably capable terrorist threat uncovered in the United States since September 11, 2001.

Krar's cyanide apparatus was only the most dramatic component of an extraordinary arsenal Krar and his common-law wife, Judith Bruey, had stashed in their Texas storage facility.

Along with the sodium cyanide, hydrochloric acid, acetic acid, and glacial acetic acid, Krar and Bruey's armory included nearly 100 assorted firearms, three machine guns, silencers, 500,000 rounds of ammunition, 60 functional pipe bombs, a remote-controlled briefcase device ready for explosive insertion, a homemade landmine, grenades, 67 pounds of Kinepak solid binary explosives (ammonium nitrate), 66 tubes of Kinepak binary liquid explosives (nitromethane), military detonators, trip wire, electric and non-electric blasting caps, and cases of military atropine syringes. (2)

The storage unit also contained an extensive library of required reading for the serious terrorist: U.S. military and CIA field manuals for improvised munitions, weapons, and unconventional warfare; handbooks on assault rifle conversions to full-auto and manufacturing silencers; formulas for poisons and chemical and biological weapons; descriptions of safety precautions in handling; and information on means of deployment. Many of the same easily acquired, open-source materials, translated into Arabic, were found in Al Qaeda terrorist manuals recovered in Afghanistan and Europe.

As for Krar's cyanide device, according to investigators, the blueprint and formula for the weapon were in the form of a computer printout and hand-written notes that Krar either took down from the internet or obtained from another source.

Margaret Kosal, an analyst of chemical and biological weapons at Stanford University's Center for International Security and Cooperation, determined that Krar had enough sodium cyanide, combined with hydrochloric acid, to produce enough hydrogen cyanide gas to kill more than 6,000 people under optimal conditions for attack.

According to Kosal, such a device, if employed in a $9 \times 40 \times 40$-foot conference room, would probably kill half of the room's occupants within one minute of inhalation. If the room was crowded, immediate fatalities could number as many as 400. More fatalities would probably follow as a result of age or ill health.

If the cyanide gas were dispersed in a larger space, say an enclosed shopping mall, hotel lobby, or school, the number of deaths would be diminished. In any case, the psychological impact on the public of a successfully deployed improvised chemical weapon in the United States would be enormous.

Kosal observed that it was not that difficult to obtain substantial amounts of sodium cyanide and acid. "While [sodium cyanide] is a DEA [Drug Enforcement Administration]-controlled compound," any notion that it "can only be acquired legally for specific agricultural or military projects is wrong," Kosal pointed out. The price of 2.5 kilograms purchased over the web "is only $105 . . . without an educational discount." (3)

In statements made to the FBI after his arrest, Krar claimed he obtained his sodium cyanide and acids from a gold-plating supply house.

FOUND BY A FLUKE

Krar's admission about how he acquired chemicals may be one of the few straightforward statements he has made to federal authorities since they stumbled upon him nearly two years ago.

On January 24, 2002, a UPS package was misdelivered to a family on Staten Island, New York. After inadvertently opening the packet, Michael Libecci discovered all array of identification documents with different names, all of which featured a photograph of the same man. Libecci turned over the packaging and its contents to the Middletown, New Jersey, police, who called the FBI in Newark.

The documents included a North Dakota birth certificate for "Anthony Louis Brach," a Social Security card for "Michael E. Brooks," a Vermont birth certificate for Brooks, a West Virginia birth certificate for "Joseph A. Curry," a Defense Intelligence Agency identification card, and a U.N. Multinational Force Observer identification card. The package was addressed to Edward S.

Feltus in Old Bridge, New Jersey. The return address was for William J. Krar at a mailbox in Tyler, Texas. Along with the bogus IDs was a letter from Krar to Feltus.

"Hope this package gets to you O.K.," wrote Krar. "We would hate to have this fall into the wrong hands."

Seven months went by before FBI agents finally talked to Feltus, a 56-year-old employee of the Monmouth County Department of Human Services. On August 8, 2002, Feltus admitted that the forged documents were intended for him, saying he wanted "an ace in the hole" against some future "disaster" or government crackdown. The documents, he said, would allow him to travel "freely in the United States."

Feltus told the agents that he was a member of the New Jersey Militia, an anti-government right-wing paramilitary group permeated with white nationalism. FBI agents later discovered that after he requested the false IDs from Krar, Feltus had stored more than 100 rifles and pistols at a fellow militia member's residence in Vermont. Seven months after the Oklahoma City bombing, leaders of the New Jersey Militia traveled to central New Hampshire on November 22, 1995, to meet with representatives from militias in Rhode Island, Massachusetts, Maine, Connecticut, and New Hampshire, to form the New England Regional Militia. Its purpose, according to the New Jersey Militia Newsletter, was to "establish an operational framework" to "develop and implement tactical contingency plans" that would include "supply, training, public relations, and intelligence gathering." (4) A key player in the New Hampshire militia at the time was William J. Krar.

NOTHING UNUSUAL?

Born in 1940, Bill Krar grew up in Connecticut, learning all about guns from his father, a gunsmith for Colt Firearms. Although he didn't serve in the military, weapons and militaria were his life's centerpiece and primary source of income. His formal education ended after a few semesters in community college. He married and had a son, but later divorced.

Exactly when Krar was drawn into the American radical-right constellation of illegal weapons dealing, shadowy paramilitaries, white nationalism, and anti-Semitic global conspiracies is unknown. According to some who knew him at the time, Krar was active in the movement by the mid-1980s. In 1984 he was dealing guns without a federal firearms license under the name of International Development Corporation (IDC) America, listed at his home address in Bedford, New Hampshire. Krar continued using IDC America as the front for his gun dealing for the next 18 years.

From 1984 to 1985, Krar was ostensibly working as a sales representative for a home-building distributorship in the nearby town of Hooksett, near Manchester. But a co-worker recalls Krar as a highly secretive man who always had a pistol at his side and stacks of *Soldier of Fortune* in his office—and who had almost no knowledge or experience of the construction business.

In an interview, this fellow employee remembered Krar and another colleague disappearing for weeks at a time, heading off to Costa Rita and other locations in Central America, even though the building supply company had no dealings beyond New England. Krar's mysterious travel activities and gun dealing occurred at the height of the Reagan administration's "private sector" paramilitary and weapons operations in support of the contras. (5)

It was also in 1985 that Krar was arrested by New Hampshire state police and charged with impersonating a police officer. He entered a no-contest plea, paid a fine, and was released. Three years later, in 1988, the building supply company where Krar worked went out of business following a fire that destroyed its building. That same year, Krar stopped filing federal income taxes and effectively dropped out of the system.

In April 1995 Krar became the subject of an FBI-Bureau of Alcohol, Tobacco, and Firearms (ATF) investigation stemming from a thwarted kidnapping and bombing plot concocted by white supremacist paramilitaries in Tennessee.

Following the arrest of Timothy McVeigh, Sean Patrick Bottoms and his brother Brian became outraged by media coverage of the Oklahoma City bomber and plotted to kidnap or kill Nashville television newscaster John Siegenthaler, now with MSNBC. (6)

After an informant tipped law enforcement to the plot, the Bottoms brothers fled to east Texas, where they were arrested on April 30, 1995. During a search of the brothers' residences, FBI and ATF agents found pipe bombs, large amounts of explosives, illegal weapons, thousands of rounds of ammunition, and a business card for "William J. Kaar" of IDC America. When questioned, Sean Bottoms told agents that "William Kaar" was in fact William J. Krar. Bottoms said he had lived in Manchester in late 1994 and early 1995 and had used Krar's IDC address on his driver's license.

After his indictment on explosives charges, Bottoms said that Krar, using the alias "Bill Franco," was active in the militia movement and that Krar said he had known about the Oklahoma City bombing before it happened. Krar had also said there were more attacks to come.

In July 1995, ATF agents questioned Krar, who told them that all he had done was sell some ammo and military surplus to Bottoms. Bottoms was then given a polygraph examination, which he failed.

Krar continued his involvement with the militia movement in New England. He later told FBI agents that this was when he first obtained sodium cyanide and began working with it, though there is no evidence to support the claim.

In a separate but simultaneous FBI-ATF investigation in Boston, Krar was under scrutiny for his role in a militia with "strong/violent antigovernment views." According to an FBI affidavit, a federal law enforcement source advised that Krar was a "white supremacist due to the anti-Semitic and anti-black literature" seen at his IDC America business in Manchester, where Krar hosted militia meetings. The source went on to say that Krar was "a good source of covert weaponry for white supremacist and anti-government militia groups."

Bruey, who was president of Krar's IDC operation at the time, told an undercover federal agent of her hatred of "U.S. government policies toward its citizens" and that she believed the government was afraid "military surplus would end up in the hands of citizens rejecting their government."

Despite this report and evidence from the Bottoms case that Krar was illegally selling firearms without a federal license, Krar and Bruey were left free to soldier on until they ran afoul of federal agents in 2001. (7)

SELF-STORE STOCKPILES

For a decade Krar conducted his operations out of multiple mail drops and storage units. According to investigators, he had no permanent shop, but would work in the storage units, running in electrical cords to power his tools and run lights. In June 2001 there was a fire at one of the two self-storage facilities Krar and Bruey were using in New Hampshire. Firemen discovered that Krar's unit contained thousands of rounds of ammunition and numerous firearms. ATF agents were called in and found among the weapons an assault rifle converted to full-auto. Krar said the weapons and ammo were the property of his employer, Ed Cunningham of Eagle Eye Guns, who had a federal firearms license. Krar and Bruey packed up the weapons and ammo and left, moving their stockpiles to another self-storage unit.

The manager of the new storage facility, Jennifer Gionet, recalled Krar vividly, describing him as "wicked anti-American."

According to an FBI affidavit, Gionet said that Krar told her "the U.S. government was corrupt" and that he "hated [it] and all of the cops." Krar went on to say he "hated Americans because they are 'money-hungry grubs.'" He also told Gionet he had several businesses in Costa Rita and offered to set her up with some "financial investments" down there. On September 11, 2001, Krar told Gionet that he knew the attacks in New York and Washington were going to happen and that there would be more in Los Angeles or Manchester. Gionet immediately reported this conversation to the local police, who notified the FBI.

Having drawn the ATF's attention in June, Bruey and Krar moved their operations to Flint, Texas, in October 2001. A young woman, Dawn Philbrick, who had become Krar's lover, accompanied them. Bruey rented two units at Noonday Storage, opened a mail drop at Mail Boxes Etc., and rented a secluded rural house. Krar was soon back at work in one of the storage units fabricating explosive devices and silencers and converting assault rifles to machine guns. He was also fabricating hundreds of magazines and receivers for Bushmaster Firearms in Maine, manufacturer of the civilian models of the AR-15 assault rifle, one of whose weapons was used by John Mohammed and Lee Malvo, the D.C. sniper team. Krar had done similar work for Bushmaster since at least 1998.

On his home computer, Krar was applying another of his skills—counterfeiting identification documents for his compatriots in the antigovernment paramilitary underground. He was as accomplished with counterfeiting as he was with guns and bombs. Over the years Krar used at least seven aliases with four different Social Security numbers and numerous business fronts. Some he used in the gun trade, some within the anti-government movement or offshore.

According to investigators, Krar didn't sell counterfeit documents on the open market but gave them away to others in the white supremacist and anti-government movements. It is not known how many sets of documents Krar distributed.

The investigation into Krar and his bogus IDs was slow in developing. It took the FBI until November 2002, 10 months after opening the case, to begin surveillance on Krar, even though they had his address.

BUSTED . . . FOR DRUGS

His activities were being monitored when, on January 11, 2003, Krar was arrested by a Tennessee state trooper in the course of a routine traffic stop on the outskirts of Nashville. Searching Krar's rental car, Trooper William Gregory found a plastic bag containing "seven marijuana cigarettes, one syringe of unknown substance, one white bottle with an unknown white substance, 40 wine-like bottles of unknown liquid," as well as two pistols, 16 knives, a stun gun, a smoke grenade, three military-style atropine injections, 260 rounds of ammunition, handcuffs, thumb cuffs, fuse ropes, binoculars, and "other various close hand-to hand combat items." Gregory also found Krar's passport, a birth certificate, a California credit union card for "William Fritz Hoffner," and a Christian missionary identification card with Krar's photo and the name "W. F. Hoffner." There were also other documents, letters to IDC America, and four pages of what appeared to be a clandestine operations plan for cross-country travel and communications. Gregory busted Krar on marijuana possession, took him into custody, and impounded the car.

The Tennessee state police then called the local FBI, which in turn contacted its Tyler, Texas officer to inform him that Krar had been arrested. Nashville FBI Special Agent David McIntosh, who interviewed Krar that day in the local jail, said that Krar told the FBI that the weapons and ammo were his and that the other material was part of his stock as a gun dealer who worked gun shows. Krar said he was moving back to New Hampshire to help his girlfriend get out of a bad divorce, and that he didn't know that the bag contained marijuana—that it was something a waitress had left beside his plate that he had just stuffed into his pocket. (8)

Krar bonded out of jail the next day, leaving his property behind, and drove west out of Nashville. Trooper Gregory opened the jar of white powder, took a whiff, assumed it was cocaine, and threw it into an evidence locker. After the discovery of Krar's chemical weapon four months later, the powder was brought to the FBI lab, where it tested positive as sodium cyanide. Federal authorities have not released information as to what liquid was found in the 40 wine bottles.

Neither Krar nor Bruey gave up any information following their arrest. Krar accepted a plea agreement on possession of a chemical weapon in exchange for Bruey getting a lighter sentence—five years. Otherwise, all the leads federal agents were able to generate were through documents obtained in the searches of Krar and Bruey's storage units, house, and vehicles. The FBI and Justice Department say the case is still under investigation.

THE FACE OF TERROR

Krar was no mere "yarn-spinner," as his defense attorney once portrayed him. The federal agents and prosecutors who interviewed Krar described him as highly intelligent, dedicated, well organized, extremely manipulative, and very dangerous. His radical right, anti-government commitment clearly grew out of the gun and paramilitary culture that spread rapidly following the Gun Control Act of 1968 and the white backlash to civil rights that arose the same year.

Krar carried copies of *Hunter* and *The Turner Diaries,* the fictional ur-texts for white American revolution and terrorism written by the late neo-Nazi William L. Pierce under the pseudonym Andrew McDonald. The books have been favorites of white nationalist and anti-government terrorists for more than two decades. McVeigh carried stacks of the *Diaries* with him during his army days and later sold them at gun shows, pressing copies into the hands of potential allies in the years running up to the Oklahoma City bombing. When federal agents searched McVeigh accomplice Terry Nichols's home in Kansas after the bombing, they found copies of the *Diaries* and *Hunter.*

Krar had a copy of *Hunter* with him when he was stopped in Nashville. *The Turner Diaries* was found in his Texas storage unit along with all four volumes of Henry Ford's classic anti-Semitic conspiracy text, *The International Jew,* and Holly Sklar's left-wing expose of the "new world order," *Trilateralism.* Like McVeigh, Krar drew his anti-government worldview from across the spectrum of right and left.

A terrorist with limited resources would probably consider Krar's chemical weapon an attractive tool. The equipment needed is simple, and the chemicals are readily available from chemical supply houses. Procedures are easily obtained in the open literature, including on the internet. Unlike the more stringent requirements for production of satin or other nerve agents, fabricating hydrogen cyanide devices demands no greater skills beyond those needed to construct an ammonium nitrate-anhydrous hydrazine truck bomb like that used in Oklahoma City.

There is no doubt that Krar was capable of producing such devices. He had the means and technical information to do so. He was well organized, disciplined, highly skilled, and comfortable in the production of improvised explosive devices.

Would he have used such a weapon? FBI agents and Justice officials who interviewed Krar don't think so. But their assessment is not reassuring.

"I don't believe Krar would've used this himself," said Brit Featherston, assistant U.S. attorney and Justice's anti-terrorism coordinator for the Eastern District of Texas. But, "If Krar came across a Tim McVeigh or an Eric Rudolph [now facing trial for fatal bombings at the Atlanta Olympics and an abortion clinic] it would be a disaster. I don't believe he'd have a problem with putting this into their hands and sending them on their way." (9)

FBI Special Agent Bart LaRocca, lead agent in the Krar investigation, agrees. "Krar was a facilitator and a provider," said LaRocca. "There was no indication that he was marketing his bombs or chemical devices. They were intended to be used against the government or in the event of 'martial law.' They were for those willing to use them or those he could manipulate into using them." (10)

An attack with such a weapon on an office building, an abortion clinic, a large auditorium, or a shopping mall could be managed by a single, disciplined individual. A terrorist cell armed with several devices could deliver a coordinated attack at different locations. Either scenario would have a tremendous psychological impact that would go far beyond immediate casualties. The bombings in Oklahoma City and during the Atlanta Olympics are stark examples of how homegrown terrorists are just as willing to indiscriminately kill men, women, and children as are their radical Islamic counterparts elsewhere in the world.

Ashcroft's Justice Department has shown almost no interest in what was, until the calamitous events of September 11, the primary domestic terrorism threat—the white nationalist, anti-government militia movement and its corollaries with theocratically driven terrorism, primarily abortion-related assassinations and bombings.

The upheavals in U.S. counter-terrorism and anti-terrorist intelligence agencies after the 2001 attacks on the World Trade Center and the Pentagon have not resulted in more nimble thinking about domestic terrorist threats. Apart from the FBI's longtime obsession with environmental and animal rights extremists, the Bureau's primary target for surveillance, investigation, and detention seems to be either immigrants of Arab descent or those who profess Islam as their religion. Although this focus is understandable, it is not commendable.

Had a similar sodium cyanide device been found in a storage unit rented by someone named Khalid or Omar, there is little doubt that Ashcroft and Mueller would have conducted a press conference and that it would have been the story of the week. For some reason, the Krar case was not deemed important—even though the facts of the case show that no other case has demonstrated a comparable and immediate threat. Certainly not the case of Jose Padilla, the small-time thug who merely talked in vague terms about a radiological bomb, or that of the young Muslims who thought it might be a good idea to travel to Pakistan for jihad training. Those incidents have been front page fodder, touted by the FBI as cases involving "significant" terrorism. Homegrown terrorists with functional cyanide gas devices are surely as serious a threat.

While Al Qaeda has no need to reach out to indigenous terrorist cells within the United States—or vice versa—a tactical confluence between them would not be surprising. Many anti-government extremists hold beliefs compatible with Islamic terrorist factions worldwide. They are violenty against the "new world order," especially with regard to U.S. government and corporate policies. They are uniformly anti-Semitic or anti-Israel and are totally opposed to the war in Iraq. (11)

Apart from the one-off attack in September 2001 by 19 young foreigners, most of them Saudis, the country's most deeply entrenched and most persistent domestic terrorist threat has come from within its own borders and at the hands of its own citizens. It would be folly to believe that the American terrorist underground, after 15 years of sustained and bloody action, has somehow just given up and disappeared.

Perhaps Ashcroft and Mueller called no press conferences because the discovery of Krar's arsenal was a fluke. It was not the result of a proactive federal anti-terrorism intelligence effort targeting the American right-wing paramilitary movement.

Just like Ashcroft and the FBI, the press thinks of "angry white guys" like McVeigh, Nichols, and Rudolph as old news.

Well, maybe Bill Krar and his compatriots don't fit the politically marketable paradigm, the post-9/11 face and faith of terrorism—non-white and Muslim. But such thinking may prove unnecessarily fatal in times to come. Consider the Krar case fair warning.

NOTES

(1) Affidavit of FBI Special Agent Leslie Lahr, United States of America v. Joseph Konopka, Case No. 02CR, March 9, 2002.

(2) Plea Agreement, United States of America v. William J. Krar, Case No. 6:03CR36, November 13, 2003; Plea Agreement, United States of America v. Judith L. Bruey, Case No. 6:03CR36 (02), November 7, 2003.

(3) Interview and e-mail exchanges with Margaret E. Kosal, July 6, 2004.

(4) *New Jersey Militia Newsletter,* January 1996.

(5) Interview with former co-worker of William Krar, August 26, 2004.

(6) Interview with John Siegenthaler, August 20, 2004.

(7) Affidavit of PB1 Special Agent Bart LaRocca, United States of America v. William J. Krar, Case No. 6:03M12, April 3, 2003.

(8) Interview with FBI Special Agent David McIntosh, Nashville, Tennessee, July 20, 2004.

(9) Interview with Brir Featherston, assistant U.S. attorney, Tyler, Texas, August 4, 2004.

(10) Interviews with FBI Special Agent Bart LaRocca, Tyler, Texas, July 7, July 22, 2004.

(11) Michael Reynolds, "Virtual Reich," *Playboy,* February 2002.

UNUSUAL SUSPECTS?

March 2000—Larry Ford, biochemist, gynecologist, and anti-government paramilitary activist, kills himself in his suburban southern California home, where police find buried caches of machine guns, assault rifles, thousands of rounds of ammunition, C-4 explosives, and canisters of ricin. In Ford's refrigerators agents discover 266 vials of assorted pathogens including salmonella, cholera, botulism, and typhoid. Ford also seemed to have some kind of working relationship with South Africa's apartheid-era bioweapons program, Project Coast.

November 2000—James Dalton Bell, anti-government militant and MIT-trained chemist, violates his parole and is charged with threatening Internal Revenue Service (IRS) agents. Bell had been convicted and sentenced to prison in 1998 on charges of attacking a Portland, Oregon, IRS office with a "stink bomb." While searching Bell's home lab, federal agents find three assault rifles, explosives, sodium cyanide, and precursor chemicals for the production of sarin nerve gas. Bell claims he had successfully manufactured a small amount of sarin. On one of Bell's computers authorities find the names and home addresses of more than 100 IRS and FBI agents along with those of local law enforcement personnel.

October 2001—Envelopes containing high-grade anthrax are mailed to a tabloid media office in Boca Raton, Florida, to major media offices in New York City, and to two Democratic senators' offices in Washington, D.C. Five die and scores are hospitalized. Although the case remains unsolved, some investigators believe the primary suspect or suspects are likely from within the American anti-government extremist movement.

March 2002—Joseph Konopka, a 25-year-old anarcho-hacker and anti-government extremist, is arrested in Chicago and charged with possession of a chemical weapon, sodium cyanide.

October 2002—Members of the Idaho Mountain Boys, an anti-government paramilitary group, are charged with possession of machine guns, plotting to kill a federal judge and a police officer, and helping fellow members escape from jail. The leader of the group, Larry Eugene Raugust, is also charged with possessing numerous bombs and booby-trap devices. Raugust is one of the leaders of the U.S. Theater Command, a nationwide militia network formed in 1997.

April 2003—William J. Krar, Judith Bruey, and Edward Feltus are arrested after Krar's weapons and chemical weapon cache are found in a Texas storage facility. Krar and Bruey are charged with possession of a chemical weapon.

October 2003—Norman Somerville, a 44-year-old anti-government militiaman is arrested. Near his rural Michigan home agents find an underground bunker stocked with 13 machine guns, thousands of rounds of ammunition, hundreds of pounds of gunpowder, and manuals on guerrilla warfare, "booby traps," and explosives. On the walls are pictures of President George W. Bush and Defense Secretary Donald Rumsfeld with the crosshairs of a rifle scope drawn over them. Somerville had also outfitted his van and Jeep Cherokee with machine guns. Somerville and his comrades had planned to use these "war wagons" in attacks on law enforcement agents. The men had been spurred by the killing of fellow militia member Scott Woodring in a shootout with police, who were attempting to arrest him for the shooting death of a state trooper. At the time of his arrest, Somerville warns of a "quiet civil war" brewing in rural Michigan. On August 10, 2004, Somerville pleads guilty to possession of machine guns and pledges "to cooperate in the hunt for shadowy rebels." Two other members of his group also enter guilty pleas to federal weapons charges.

June 2004—A Bureau of Alcohol, Tobacco, and Firearms (ATF) raid uncovers a cache of castor beans, formulas for extracting ricin from the beans, and bomb-making materials in the suburban apartment of Boston-area anti-government activist Michael Crooker. Crooker, once convicted for fraud and possession of a machine gun, had come under scrutiny by the U.S. Postal Service for shipping a silencer to a compatriot in Ohio.

July 2004—After his arrest in south Florida in November 2003, Michael Crooker. John Jordi, a Christian anti-abortion zealot and ex-U.S. Army Ranger, is sentenced to five years in prison for plotting to bomb abortion clinics, gay bars, and certain churches. U.S. District Judge James Cohn rules that Jordi is not a terrorist because federal laws require that plots have an international component to be considered terrorism.

August 2004—Two young Tennessee leaders of a dozen-member anti-government paramilitary cell called the American Independence Group (AIG) are charged with attempted bank robbery and possession of assault weapons. The AIG had intended to use the money from the bank robbery to fund their operations. According to federal agents, the AIG hated the federal government and select ethnic groups and talked of declaring war on law enforcement and killing President Bush.

Also in August, a 66-year-old convicted counterfeiter and antigovernment activist, Gale Nettles, is charged with plotting to build an ammonium nitrate/fuel oil truck bomb and use it to attack the federal courthouse in Chicago. According to federal agents, Nettles had stored 500 pounds of ammonium nitrate in a Chicago-area storage facility and was seeking more from an FBI informant. The informant also stated that Nettles was looking to make contact with either Al Qaeda or Hamas.

Michael Reynolds writes on political and religious extremism and terrorism. He has contributed to Playboy, U.S. News & World Report, Rolling Stone, 60 Minutes, *and* Newsweek. *He was senior analyst at the Southern Poverty Law Center's Intelligence Project from 1994 to 2000.*

13

The Growing Threat of Home-Grown Terrorism

After Another S.D. Attack, the Anti-Business ELF Shows Why It Is as Dangerous as Bin Laden

Elan Journo

As we combat Islamic terrorism abroad, we must recognize the deadly threat posed by a homegrown source—one that since 1997 has been responsible for over 600 attacks and has inflicted more than $100 million in property damage.

The attacks have become bolder and more fierce. In August a 206-unit apartment complex in San Diego was firebombed, resulting in $50 million in damage. And just days ago, also in San Diego, four upscale homes under construction were torched. This growing danger is: environmental terrorism. It is time that we reflect on the scale of the danger we face—and the ideology behind that menace.

From Alabama to Michigan, from Pennsylvania to California, underground cells of eco-terrorists have been waging a campaign of tree-spiking, industrial sabotage, arson, and bombing. Last year the most prominent eco-terrorist group, the Earth Liberation Front, proudly claimed responsibility for more than 130 attacks. What is their goal?

According to the ELF, our westernized way of life "comes at the expense of . . . the natural environment." By seeking a safer, longer, happier life—by seeking more than a bare, primitive subsistence—mankind, they say, is guilty of crimes against nature. Accordingly, they wish "to inflict economic damage on those profiting from the destruction and exploitation of the natural environment"—hoping eventually "to speed up the collapse of industry."

Eco-terrorists have consistently targeted these "exploiters"—from timber companies, to land developers, to scientific researchers. In the most notorious

San Diego Business Journal, Sept 29, 2003, v24, i39, p47(1).
"The Growing Threat of Home-Grown Terrorism" by Elan Journo. © 2003 CBJ, L.P.

of their actions, in Vail, Colo., in 1998, the ELF burned down part of a ski resort, causing $12 million in property damage. The attack was mounted, the group said, on behalf of the wildlife whose habitat was being "trespassed" upon.

GLOATING LIKE BIN LADEN

Last year nine new homes in Phoenix were firebombed because they were deemed, by eco-terrorists, to be encroaching on the natural desert. Two years ago, to protest the existence of Huntingdon Life Sciences, a British animal-research lab, "animal liberationist" goons blew up several cars belonging to the firm's employees, and severely beat the company's managing director with baseball bats.

These militants are alarmingly brazen. Gloating in a tone redolent of Osama bin Laden's post-Sept. 11 videos, the ELF has published a meticulous, 47-page report of its self-described illegal activities. The attacks are listed by region, date, tactics used, and damage caused.

There are even mock awards for the "most impressive" attacks and "most vehicles damaged in a single action." To spur further violence, the group's Web site offers a free illustrated manual on "Setting Fires With Electrical Timers" (along with advice on what to do if an FBI agent comes knocking).

Astonishingly, little has been done to stop the eco-terrorists. Some have been caught and even brought before grand juries, but few have been punished. In February 2002, the House Resources Subcommittee held a hearing on eco-terrorism, but nothing came of it: the main witness, an ELF spokesman, refused to answer most of the questions.

IS KILLING NEXT?

Meanwhile, the attacks, both large and small, continued last year at an average pace of one every four days. These people are not mere vandals. They declare that they do not "consider the destruction of property to be committing violence" if done for the sake of nature. It is just a matter of time before they extend their rabid rationalizations to the killing of human beings.

The eco-terrorists hate the system of capitalism and industrialization because it leads us, properly, to regard nature as only a means to satisfy man's wishes. They are driven by an ideology that regards human life as dispensable whenever it impedes their goal of keeping nature untouched. With every dam he constructs, every house he erects and every shovelful of soil he removes, man is denounced for "raping the earth" and "murdering the ecosystem."

The eco-terrorists want to stop all such activities—by whatever means necessary.

Our inaction in the face of Islamic terrorists before Sept. 11 helped to embolden them; our inaction in the face of eco-terrorism is doing the same. We dare not wait for eco-terrorists, motivated by their own nihilistic ideology, to mount their own Sept. 11. They must be stopped by the force of government, now.

Journo is a senior writer for the Ayn Rand Institute in Irvine.

14

America's Homegrown Terrorists

Brandon Bosworth

Enron CEO Kenneth Lay wasn't the only one pleading the Fifth Amendment on Capitol Hill in February. Testifying on February 13 before a House committee investigating terrorism committed in the U.S. in the name of environmentalism, former Earth Liberation Front (ELF) spokesman Craig Rosebraugh invoked the right against self-incrimination over 50 times. He even took the Fifth when asked if he was a U.S. citizen. At one point Representative George Nethercutt (RWA) jokingly asked if Mr. Rosebraugh was "in any way related" to Mr. Lay. As you might have guessed, Rosebraugh took the Fifth on that one, too.

Craig Rosebraugh hasn't always been so hesitant to speak his mind. A scrawny, bespectacled 28-year-old with a shaved head, he first became involved with ELF and its sister group the Animal Liberation Front (ALF) in 1997. He claims the organizations contacted him anonymously with assorted statements and communiques, which he then prepared as press releases. These releases were sent to the media, and Mr. Rosebraugh made himself available for interviews and speeches. Who exactly were these shadowy people Mr. Rosebraugh was representing? ELF first reared its ugly head in England in 1992. By 1997 it had begun to operate in America. There are no formal headquarters or known internal structure, and most of its members seem to be high school or college students. But over the years, both ELF and ALF have been responsible for many serious acts of ecoterrorism. According to James Jarboe, the FBI's top domestic terrorism officer, they are "the most active" and "cause the most damage" of any U.S. terrorist organization. He estimates

The American Enterprise, April-May 2002, v13, i3, p48(2).
"America's Homegrown Terrorists" by Brandon Bosworth. © 2002 American Enterprise Institute for Public Policy Research.

that ELF and ALF have caused $43 million in damage over the years. One of the most costly acts was the 1998 torching of a ski resort in Vail, Colorado that caused $12 million in damages. In 1999, ELF members set fire to Michigan State University's Agriculture Hall to destroy academic research they found offensive. A million dollars of damage was done to a Eugene, Oregon car dealership when enviro-terrorists destroyed 36 trucks and SUVs. Last year, ALF firebombed the Coulston Foundation biomedical facility in New Mexico, causing another $1 million in damages.

There's more. In his testimony to Congress, Richard Berman, executive director of the Center for Consumer Freedom, explained that "during the past three years, ELF and ALF have claimed responsibility for smashing bank windows, torching a chicken feed truck, burning a horse corral at a Bureau of Land Management facility . . . even setting bombs under meat delivery trucks." He noted that ELF and ALF took joint credit for the firebombing of a Tucson, Arizona McDonald's that occurred, ironically, on September 11, 2001. Mr. Berman estimates these groups are responsible for "well over 1,000 documented criminal acts in the U.S." ELF and ALF themselves admit to committing 137 illegal acts in North America in 2001 (25 since September 11), causing millions of dollars in damages.

Throughout their terror campaign, ELF and ALF could always count on the support of Craig Rosebraugh. He shrugs off the idea that he represented vandals, saying "if we are vandals, so were those who destroyed forever the gas chambers of Buchenwald and Auschwitz." Mr. Rosebraugh defends the burning of a luxury home in Boulder, Colorado on the grounds that "there is no reason . . . for someone to have . . . a multimillion-dollar home when there are people living in the same city who can't afford proper shelter." Do ELF and ALF expect to win new converts through terrorism? "That's not the immediate goal" according to Craig Rosebraugh. "The immediate goal is to cause economic damage."

As for the possibility of "physical harm that may come to the public," Mr. Rosebraugh says ELF and ALF "pose no threat, and they never have posed any threat." He claims "no one has ever been injured by the group's many actions." But he has encouraged others "to find a local Earth raper and make them pay. . . . Furriers, meat packers, bosses, developers, rich industry leaders are all Earth rapers." Though Mr. Rosebraugh left out journalists, at least one of them has also been "made to pay" for alleged crimes against nature. British journalist Graham Hall, who made a documentary critical of ALF, was kidnapped at gunpoint in October 1999. Using a branding iron, his captors branded the letters "ALF"—each letter four inches high—onto his back. An ALF spokesman explained that "People who make their living this way have to expect from time to time to take the consequences of their actions."

More mainstream environmental groups have put some distance between themselves and ELF and ALF. Greenpeace executive director John Passacatando issued a statement reading, "If we define eco-terrorism as violence, violence to people or to property, we disavow it." Sierra Club spokesman Allen

Mattison believes that by using property destruction as a tool, ELF and ALF are "alienating potential allies." How does Craig Rosebraugh feel about these criticisms? "Many individuals in the environmental community despise the ELF and its tactics out of some learned hypocritical white liberalism."

What would lead a vegan baker like Craig Rosebraugh into the arms of America's most damaging homegrown terrorists? While he didn't say anything to Congress besides "I'll take the Fifth," Rosebraugh did submit 11 pages of written testimony that sheds further light on his thinking. He claims to have been a patriotic, mainstream youth up until the Gulf War. Then Mr. Rosebraugh was "horrified at the slaughter of Iraqi civilians by the U.S. military" and became involved with the anti-war movement. That's when he "began to understand the disastrous relationship our modern society has with many animal nations." From there it was a short hop to left-wing revisionist history, in which "the origins of this country were based upon murder, exploitation, and ultimate genocide."

Rosebraugh now believes the "so-called 'Great American Revolution'" really "only served and benefited the privileged white male." And terrorism? In Rosebraugh's mind, "the U.S. government by far has been the most extreme terrorist organization in planetary history." His rambling screed ends with "ALL POWER TO THE PEOPLE. LONG LIVE THE EARTH LIBERATION FRONT. LONG LIVE THE ANIMAL LIBERATION FRONT. LONG LIVE ALL THE SPARKS ATTEMPTING TO IGNITE THE REVOLUTION. SOONER OR LATER THE SPARKS WILL TURN INTO A FLAME!"

Not nearly enough is being done to blunt eco-terrorism. University labs, medical and agricultural researchers, loggers, homebuilders, pharmaceutical companies, and others are now attacked with regularity. The fact that Congress finally held hearings in February is a good sign, but more needs to be done. It is shameful that there have been hardly any arrests for the countless crimes the ELF and ALF have been responsible for. Partly because these attacks are not widely reported in the media, there has been relatively little public outcry against eco-terrorists. Even before September 11 if you said the word "terrorist" to the average American, the first thing to pop into his mind would be an image of some bearded, unkempt Arab; not a middle-class white kid. Terrorists came from overseas, not from Oregon.

While nothing ELF or ALF have done so far comes close to the magnitude of the attacks on the World Trade Center, how long will that remain true? Should we ignore these bombers, burglars, arsonists, and saboteurs among us because they remind some people of the romanticized radicals of the Baby Boomers' adolescence? For those who shrug off these junior terrorists, Representative Scott McInnis (R-CO) has a warning: "It would be a mistake to call them misguided youth, or trust-fund babies with nothing to do. They are hardened criminals."

Brandon Bosworth is a TAE associate editor.

IV

ISSUES IN HOMELAND SECURITY

In 2002, Congress enacted the Homeland Security Act to protect America against the growing threat of international and domestic terrorism. The newly established federal Department of Homeland Security is charged with protecting America's critical infrastructure against attacks. An especially important tool in the law enforcement arsenal against terrorism is the federal USA PATRIOT Act of 2001 that provides tools required to thwart preparations of future terrorist attacks. Critics, however, fear a steady erosion of Civil Rights in response to attempts to battle terrorism.

15

The Homeland Security Bureaucracy

Eli Lehrer

WHEN a nation seeking to protect itself finds diplomacy, war, and foreign intelligence gathering insufficient, it can undertake three other types of activities to defend itself. It can control the movement of potential terrorists entering the country or traveling within it; it can capture or neutralize terrorist plotters within its borders; and when all else fails, it can mitigate damage from terrorist attacks. These three activities—access control, law enforcement, and disaster mitigation—comprise the essentials of homeland security. Congress and the Bush administration have consolidated many federal efforts to accomplish these three tasks in the Department of Homeland Security (DHS). In so doing they hope to protect the nation from future terrorist attacks.

Certainly, much good work has been accomplished. But thus far, not enough thought has been given to the considerable structural impediments to serious reform. DHS's vast reach coupled with its lack of bodies on the ground, the checkered history of American bureaucratic reform, and the difficulty DHS's constituent agencies have encountered defining new missions all suggest that homeland security is at best a work in progress. DHS's various bureaus are still too limited in scope, too committed to their legacy missions, and too unlikely to change for the existence of a Department of Homeland Security to modify the way America confronts terrorists.

Public Interest, Summer 2004, i156, p71(15).

THE DIRECTORATES

DHS carries out an enormous number of duties. At the highest level of its organizational chart, DHS consists of four collections of related programs called directorates: Border and Transportation Security (BTS); Emergency Preparedness and Response (EPR); Science and Technology (S & T); Information Analysis and Infrastructure Protection (IAIP); and Management. The Coast Guard, U.S. Citizenship Service and Immigration Service (which issues visas and grants citizenship), the Secret Service, and the new Office of State and Local Coordination (which administers grants) all report directly to the Secretary of Homeland Security. Outside of the Management Directorate, which handles payroll, computer systems, and human resources, DHS's major programs were all transferred from other agencies.

All of the directorates carry out varied missions. The Border and Transportation Security Directorate has the biggest budget and the highest public profile. It includes the Transportation Security Administration (TSA) and two border agencies created from pieces of the Border Guard, Customs Service, Agricultural Inspection Service, and Immigration and Naturalization Service. The first, Immigration and Customs Enforcement (ICE), enforces immigration law within the borders of the United States by catching people in the country illegally. Customs and Border Protection is the second; it secures the borders. More than half of all DHS employees work for the Border and Transportation Security Directorate, and over 70 percent of these work as baggage screeners. The Federal Emergency Management Agency (FEMA), which dominates the Emergency Preparedness and Response Directorate, serves four functions. It funds rebuilding after disasters, offers expert advice on preparing for disasters before they happen, gives operating and capital assistance to local emergency response agencies, and runs some secret facilities designed to help the federal government survive a catastrophic attack. Emergency Preparedness and Response also administers a vaccine stockpile program transferred from the Department of Health and Human Services and programs intended to mitigate nuclear, chemical, and biological attacks formerly belonging to the FBI and Department of Energy. The Science and Technology Directorate is DHS's smallest: It runs four major labs that mostly concern themselves with developing countermeasures for weapons of mass destruction. It also funds university research.

The Information Analysis and Infrastructure Protection Directorate, on the other hand, attempts to improve our handle on information about terrorist threats, drawing together six separate programs from agencies ranging from the FBI to the Department of Energy. It runs the much-derided color-coded warning system, and produces the daily Homeland Security briefing for the president. It creates the briefing by analyzing information from the nominally independent Terrorist Threat Integration Center (TTIC) created by the president in January 2003. This center—theoretically a joint venture between the FBI, CIA, and DHS—has a staff drawn largely from the CIA and is housed at

CIA headquarters. DHS's top officials are not always privy to the sources and methods the center uses to develop the reports they receive from it. With a few minor exceptions, mostly related to the Internet, the directorate's programs do not attempt to gather information itself.

FIGUREHEAD?

Federal homeland security activities cover only a small part of the law enforcement and disaster mitigation continuum. Even access control functions, which the federal government dominates in some areas, have a more federalist tinge than many assume. DHS's scope, in other words, provides evidence against those who believe it will make a major difference in the way America carries out homeland security tasks. The lack of national reach is distressing because homeland security is a quintessentially national task. Terrorist attacks can happen almost anywhere, will likely hit nationally prominent targets, and will almost certainly overwhelm the resources of local governments.

A majority of people involved in the law enforcement functions associated with homeland security do not work for DHS. Many terrorist plots will arise in America's neighborhoods, and DHS could never simultaneously monitor all possible sources of terrorist attack. Fewer than 15 percent of all law-enforcement personnel in the United States work for the federal government, and less than half of these work for DHS. The United States has 17,000 police agencies—more than all other developed countries put together. None of these agencies has a legal obligation to take tactical guidance—much less strategic cues—from the federal government. DHS, in any case, stations nearly all of its employees in Washington, at major airports and along the borders. It has no presence in over three quarters of America's counties. Even within the federal government, many agencies involved in what everyone agrees are homeland security functions remain outside DHS. In addition to the Terrorist Threat Integration Center, the FBI, which leads intelligence gathering, the Drug Enforcement Administration, which tracks a key source of terrorist financing, and the Bureau of Alcohol, Tobacco, Firearms, and Explosives, which would play a major role in contingencies involving bombs or chemical weapons, remain outside DHS. These agencies, furthermore, have missions that mention fighting terrorism as only one task among many and, even if placing them within DHS had a major effect on their duties, it might also damage their ability to carry out other tasks. If the federal government plays a major role in trying to arrest terrorists, DHS will probably not lead those efforts.

Disaster mitigation, likewise, falls largely outside of DHS's scope of responsibility. While employees of the Emergency and Preparedness Response Directorate (mostly from FEMA) do show up at the scene of most major disasters and provide grants for rebuilding and mitigating, they have few "troops" on the ground. FEMA itself has only 2,600 employees—fewer than the Illinois State Police—and only about 2,000 of them can show up at even the largest disasters. Most of the responsibilities for actually taking care of people after disasters and terrorist attacks fall on state and local disaster management bureaucracies that, collectively, employ at least 10 times FEMA's personnel. New York, California, and Texas combined have more people in disaster mitigation agencies than FEMA. The agency does a superb job mitigating damage from natural disasters, but seems to have little interest in terrorism.

The federal government dominates access control tasks around the country. At borders and airports, federal agents remain in full control. Other facilities, ranging from office buildings to rocket launch pads, remain in the hands of a dizzying array of private contractors, federal bureaus, and local agencies. DHS, however, administers most of the contracts for these private security firms through the Federal Protective Service. It does not do anything to secure many prominent facilities—ranging from the Sears Tower to New York's City Hall—that have no federal offices.

It's clear that DHS's scope is far smaller than the entire task of homeland security. Given that DHS does not have direct control over much of what it is supposed to do, it comes as no surprise that a number of tasks DHS promised to perform remain undone. A national assessment of critical infrastructure—a disaster mitigation task—may take as long as five years. It was promised in one year. A repeated promise to create a single unified terrorist watch list, likewise, may never come to fruition. DHS has decided to build a complex terrorist tracking computer system instead. Access control tasks, which DHS does have far more complete control over, do appear to have proceeded more smoothly: TSA, for example, has met goals to screen every airline passenger and perform X-rays or CT scans of checked luggage, and Customs and Border Protection will eventually begin tracking foreigners visiting the United States, albeit several years behind schedule.

Some of these failings may stem from the growing pains implicit in starting a new federal agency. But their roots are likely deeper than that: DHS simply does not have the breadth of control necessary to mandate that state and local emergency managers or even other federal police agencies do what it says.

MISSIONS, OLD AND NEW

Nearly all of DHS's programs have long-standing missions that bear only a tangential relationship to fighting terrorism. Labs tasked with developing biological weapons countermeasures, for example, grew out of the Department of Agriculture and have animal and plant disease experts on staff. Customs and Border Protection draws together agriculture inspectors, border patrol officers, and members of drug enforcement details. One can see this pattern repeat itself in several of DHS's most high-profile agencies: FEMA, the Secret Service, the Federal Protective Service, Immigration and Customs Enforcement and Customs and Border Protection, Coast Guard, Citizenship and Immigration Services, the Office of State and Local Coordination, and the Transportation Security Administration. Together, these bureaus and programs spend about 80 percent of DHS's total budget and employ roughly the same percentage of its workforce. Yet homeland security remains for many of them a second-level priority.

The Federal Emergency Management Agency, which had a clear mandate before DHS's creation, now faces a multiplicity of conflicting ones. Long an unimportant agency full of campaign contributors, FEMA underwent a massive reorganization under Clinton-era administrator James Lee Witt. It emphasized providing timely mitigation assistance first and payments to every individual and government that qualified for them second. Witt thought the agency should concentrate on natural disasters. "During the 1990s," Witt told the Congressional Research Service's (CRS) Keith Bea, "FEMA has responded to over 500 emergency and major disaster related events, only two of those were related to terrorism: [the first World Trade Center bombing] and Oklahoma City." As a result of this new focus, cities could be rebuilt more quickly after natural disasters, and FEMA employees, who often managed to arrive at natural disaster sites before trouble started, took on a quasi-heroic stature helping localities organize evacuations and providing expert advice on post-disaster reconstruction.

Under DHS, however, FEMA now emphasizes "prepar[ing] to manage the consequences of terrorist attacks, especially those involving the use of weapons of mass destruction." Bea has studied the agency carefully, and raises a number of doubts about the desirability of having it join DHS. In a July 2002 CRS report, he observes that most of FEMA's programs in "emergency food and shelter, flood insurance, natural hazard mitigation, and the maintenance of data on fires, have little application to homeland security." Despite emphasizing terrorism on its web site and in executive speeches, FEMA's actual activities remain heavily invested in natural disaster mitigation and relief to the exclusion of terrorism. Although a few of its programs have new names, its largest new post-September 11 initiative (funded at $150 million in 2003 and $200 million in 2004) has been to digitize the nation's floodplain maps—a task that has almost no relationship to fighting terrorism. Only one new program, emergency management planning grants that FEMA passes directly to states with little oversight, even addresses terrorism. FEMA, in other words, has a well-defined role to play. But it does not relate to terrorism.

Despite a variety of different proposed missions, the Coast Guard has always seen itself as a small-boat navy. Its naval mystique aside, it was housed in the Treasury Department at its creation in 1915, moved into the Department of Transportation when Lyndon Johnson created it, and now resides in the Department of Homeland Security. (It transfers to the Defense Department during wartime.) The Coast Guard's official history emphasizes its role engaging German U-Boats, pirates, and Viet Cong in places the Navy couldn't go. Historically, it has resisted change. The Nixon and Reagan administrations tried to use the Coast Guard for intercepting illegal drugs, but the effort flopped and has become a low priority. Efforts to turn the Guard into a boating safety and environmental protection agency under Jimmy Carter, George H.W. Bush, and Bill Clinton had similar results. Although the agency issues two or three press releases every day, it has not mentioned a specific action against a polluter since at least 2002.

The periodic change of mission has come largely because many policy makers view the need for a small boat navy with skepticism. Despite heavy spending on military hardware, the Coast Guard has not gotten into a serious firefight since Vietnam. Under DHS, however, the Coast Guard has continued to emphasize small-time naval combat to the exclusion of other tasks. Since September 11, its budget has grown by $1 billion, or slightly more than 20 percent. Over 90 percent of the increases have gone to upgrade weapons systems and boats under the new "deepwater" program and to deploy new "Marine Safety and Security Teams"—essentially Coast Guard special forces units—to respond to terrorists. These moves may make military sense and help fight terrorism, but they move the Coast Guard in the direction of becoming a full-fledged fifth armed service rather than a national maritime police force. On the other hand, the Coast Guard has done more to inspect ships approaching U.S. ports and searching them for weapons and terrorists. It's probably too early to tell how quickly the Coast Guard will move to change its organizational focus. For the moment, its operations appear to reflect a commitment to a new task while its capital spending appears to continue its legacy as an aspiring fifth military branch.

NEW PRIORITIES?

The Secret Service also remains committed to its legacy missions—dignitary protection and counterfeiting investigation. Its new homeland security goal, first announced in 1998, is coordinating security around "National Special Security Events" such as the Olympics, but this effort appears almost stillborn. While its most recent strategic plan begins with a good deal of boilerplate about the importance of homeland security and does make an effort to attach its executive protection functions to fighting terrorism, it does not define any strategic goals related to National Security Special Events. It continues zealously to protect top officials, but the majority of Secret Service investigators still work on counterfeiting. Only a small portion of its investigative capabilities directly confronts terrorist organizations. Local police forces, likewise, rarely accept total Secret Service authority in coordinating security around designated events. This isn't altogether surprising: The Secret Service, a reasonably small agency, has neither the reach nor the expertise to serve as an allpurpose terrorism police force as it was envisioned in 1998.

Although the Federal Protective Service (FPS) employs more uniformed officers than any other federal law enforcement agency except TSA, most Americans have never heard of it. The agency provides the armed security guards—almost all of them contractors—at federal buildings. Its main task has always been responding when an alarm sounds. In all, it employs nearly 10,000 security and police personnel. It does not have a good reputation. The Justice Department, for example, kicked out FPS guards from its Washington head-quarters in the mid 1980s and now administers its own security contracts. FPS remains heavily invested in responding to alarm calls just as it was before. But as the department's founders envisioned, it does so in a broader context. It seeks to make sure that other agencies can use its MegaCenters for monitor-ing alarms in buildings and that the force does not respond on its own. This task represents the sort of interoperability DHS's creators envisioned. Its new posture makes it easier to call in police forces with better investigative person-nel and methods when something goes wrong. This is only a small step, but the Federal Protective Service appears to have begun undertaking tasks useful to a larger department.

The new United States Citizenship and Immigration Services, which as-sumes many of the functions of the Immigration and Naturalization Service, remains difficult to deal with and unresponsive to requests for customer ser-vice, even by the standards of a government agency. Perhaps this is because the agency serves immigrants who do not vote or organize politically. From the standpoint of homeland security, it appears to have made some limited progress: The travel documents issued to resident aliens returning home for a visit, which many analysts believed were a crucial weakness in America's bor-der control system, are much harder to forge than they were before Septem-ber 11. A system called the Student and Visitor Information System, or SEVIS, now tracks foreign students who come to the United States and alerts federal officials if an individual in the country on a student visa fails to attend classes.

More serious issues related to immigration and customs, however, remain unresolved. An ambitious project called U.S.-VISIT (which also involves Customs and Border Protection) would collect photographs and digital fin-gerprints from every foreigner who enters the United States, but it has moved slowly. While DHS met a vaguely worded congressional deadline to collect information about visitors, the full-fledged U.S.-VISIT computer system won't roll out nationally until at least 2006.

Customs and Border Protection and Immigration and Customs Enforce-ment, the external and internal immigration control agencies, seemed to be the easiest victory for those reorganizing the DHS bureaucracy. Former Clin-ton advisor John Podesta and former Reagan administration official Ken Duberstein were in agreement on this when they announced that agency con-solidations would help "focus the American people and the government on the mission at hand, get agencies to reorder priorities and streamline operations." The integration has not gone smoothly. Uniforms and logos from agencies that haven't existed for almost two years still predominate at airports, and reports indicate that the new agency suffers from low morale. A computer system taken mostly from the Immigration and Naturalization Service has caused significant problems. Internal bureaucratic squabbles are rife in both agencies. Fights have erupted over matters as trivial as the types of weapons agents should carry. The New Republic contends that the worst problems of the INS's notoriously unresponsive bureaucracy have infected the other agencies. Given that CPB and ICE face a dual task of integrating their component parts into new bureaus and fitting those bureaus into a new department, it is probably too early to judge the efforts' success or failure.

One major DHS component does not have a legacy mission: The Transportation Security Administration. Unlike every other major component of the Department of Homeland Security, TSA was created from scratch after September 11. It has a budget of nearly $5 billion and employs more people than the Coast Guard and FBI combined. Despite some gripes from libertarians, a few internal slip-ups, and more than a little ribbing from late-night comedians, its internal polling (conducted under contract with the consulting firm BearingPoint) has shown that the flying public likes the agency and, according to a series of Gallup Polls between 2001 and 2003, feels that airline security has improved since September 11. And terrorists have not succeeded in hijacking any airplanes. Air travel, after a sharp post-September 11 downturn, recovered nicely in 2002 and 2003, hitting an all-time high in December 2003. Judged as an economic signaling mechanism, too, the Transportation Security Administration appears to have accomplished much. Studies from BearingPoint, DHS's own inspector general, and the U.S. General Accounting Office, however, showed that TSA's actual security performance is lackluster.

Moreover, it is difficult to ascertain if the agency has prevented any attacks on airports or airlines. And when it comes to defining its mandate, the agency does not seem to have done much: Should it emphasize getting people through inspection as quickly as possible? Providing maximum security? How much attention should it devote to non-airline security missions such as securing Amtrak trains, seaports, and inter-city trucking? So far, these questions remain unanswered. The agency has a better chance of developing a mandate than nearly any other within DHS, but thus far the work of simply setting up a functioning baggage-inspection agency and developing appropriate tactics have prevented it from asking larger strategic questions.

OUTSOURCING

Since DHS itself lacks the scope to carry out its many disaster mitigation and law enforcement tasks, grant programs are a crucial component in establishing a national strategy. Although state and local grant programs employ reasonably few people and run mostly through DHS's Office of State and Local Coordination, they make up roughly 10 percent of the DHS budget. The office, created in early 2004, consolidates the overwhelming majority of DHS grants. Despite protests of underfunding from the Conference of Mayors and virtually every police chief, however, the Bush administration has not starved state and local law enforcement agencies for resources. Over the administration's three years in office, funding for first responders has grown 29 percent a year on average, which is almost exactly the same rate that overall homeland security spending has grown. This is faster than the 19 percent annual rate at which this assistance to state and local governments grew under the Clinton administration.

Despite the overall spending increase, the Bush administration has angered police agencies by cutting nearly all Clinton-era grant programs. It has made them even angrier by proposing cutting overall assistance for 2005 back to 2002 levels. The Community-Oriented Policing Services (COPS) office closely associated with Clinton's "100,000 new police officers" pledge, sustained the deepest cuts. It now does little besides publish pamphlets and fund police officers in schools. Two other grants, the population-based Local Law Enforcement Block Grants and crime-rate based Byrne Grants, have also sustained cuts.

Nearly all new federal dollars flow through DHS block grants. This approach does not help coordination between agencies or help to develop a national strategy. COPS grants, unlike the new DHS grants, were awarded on a competitive basis and could, at least in theory, serve as the basis for a national strategy. DHS grants, on the other hand, rarely have strings attached. So far, as a result, block grant programs have encouraged heavy spending on equipment coupled with modest spending on planning, coordination, and intelligence. Many grant proposals read like Christmas lists from information technology directors, and the federal-state establishment in turn plays Santa Claus. By the end of 2004, for example, nearly every major city in the country will have used federal money to buy chemical-weapons protection gear for its entire patrol force. Due to significant reductions in funding for personnel and other daily operations, they have come under increasing pressure from police agencies to use these funds to replace money that once flowed from the COPS office and other federal grant programs. Several states, including Massachusetts and California, indeed, have had to deal with accusations that local police agencies diverted homeland security funds to ordinary law enforcement tasks. The 2004 and 2005 grants from DHS, however, are more specific and less oriented towards equipment purchases than those that came before them. Many states are also becoming more stringent in the way they award grants. The consolidation of most grant programs in a single office (which DHS will complete sometime in 2005) will also make it easier for an administration so inclined to articulate a national strategy. So far, however, a massive increase in grant spending appears to have done little to establish a national homeland security strategy, although grants have armed local agencies with a wide variety of new equipment.

CRITICAL TASKS

As its long list of incomplete tasks and unmet objectives indicates, DHS is unlikely to change the way American government does business. In a comprehensive survey of managerial innovations and reorganizations in government, Louis Winnick, writing in *City Journal,* found that "genuinely radical transformations in government cannot occur without radical transformations in policy, in the fundamental 'what' of government as distinguished from the procedural 'how.'" Hoover commissions under Harry Truman and Dwight Eisenhower, Jimmy Carter's zero-based budgeting, Ronald Reagan's Grace Commission, Al Gore's Reinventing Government initiative, and the President's Management Agenda (proffered by George W. Bush) all examined the structure of federal bureaucracy and produced reams of reports. New agencies built from existing programs—the Education, Transportation and Energy departments stand out—have not transformed the federal government. None has produced large management savings, vastly improved public services, or given bureaucrats a new sense of mission.

Truly remaking a government agency's mission appears to require what James Q. Wilson calls a "critical task": a group of "behaviors, which, if successfully performed by key organizational members, would enable the organization to manage its critical environmental problem." Wilson, writing in his book *Bureaucracy*, finds that successful agencies develop a high degree of public support for the selected critical task, energize their employees in carrying it out, and receive a degree of independence necessary to discard duties peripheral to this critical task. Most programs define a critical task when Congress creates them or during a period of drastic growth. Government agencies such as the Army Corps of Engineers, and Apollo-era NASA are the ones that academics cite as models of excellence in service and accomplishment, and these have devoted themselves to single critical tasks, sometimes to the exclusion of other tasks. The Social Security Administration, for example, has a clear critical task of sending a benefit check to every American over 65. The Department of Homeland Security, in contrast, has only the large and amorphous goal of "protect[ing] the nation against further terrorist attacks."

Asking an entire cabinet level agency to find a critical task, however, probably isn't possible. As Wilson observes, any major cabinet-level department carries out a mission too diverse to fall into a single critical task. Thus, he finds, critical tasks usually come into existence at the bureau level rather than on an agency-wide level. Looking at DHS's bureaus, however, one can find little evidence that new critical tasks have emerged.

GROWING PAINS

Faced with the specter of international terrorism, the Bush administration had little choice but to create a bureaucracy to confront it. This bureaucracy has had some successes: U.S.-VISIT will make borders more secure, baggage gets inspected more stringently, and, despite a lack of progress so far, the creation of Customs and Border Protection and Immigration and Customs Enforcement at least raises the possibility that an effective system may one day exist to secure America's borders and track down criminals and terrorists from foreign countries. Behind the scenes, some glimmers of hope emerge. The Management Directorate has integrated roughly half of the department's management computer systems, a task that will deliver savings and greater organizational coherence down the road.

The vast scope of DHS's responsibilities and its failure to develop critical tasks for most of its components indicate that the new department has yet to develop a coherent national strategy. Through good management, many of its components may become more agile and effective. Still, DHS does not include some functions it probably should, such as the FBI's counter-terrorism programs. And it includes some, most prominently FEMA, that would probably do better outside of the department. Despite sending local governments vast sums of money, it has yet to articulate a strategy for dealing with many of the disaster mitigation and law enforcement tasks the federal government could never handle on its own. Of course, providing this level of strategic guidance is a delicate balancing act. While the federal government needs to provide advice and assistance to local agencies, any effort to specify tactics and strategies for non-terrorism-related matters could damage a local policing system that is arguably the best in the world.

Many of DHS's early growing pains were probably unavoidable. Nobody expected 22 diffuse agencies to merge seamlessly just because Congress and the president wanted them to. So far, however, it seems the department still has much to do in its quest to make America safer.

16

The Controversy About U.S. Policies

Authors, Whistleblowers Decry Flawed U.S. Policies in War on Terror

Glenn Garvin

LOS ANGELES—From security lapses to unsound foreign policy to out-moded rescue equipment, the U.S. government has done almost nothing to repair the problems that led to the Sept. 11 attacks, and another catastrophic terrorist strike is virtually inevitable, a panel of government whistleblowers and investigative journalists warned Sunday.

Angrily denouncing what he called "the whitewashing of the people who did bring you 9-11 through their negligence and dereliction of duty," former CIA counterterrorism analyst Michael Scheuer predicted government inaction and cover-up will lead to "another 30,000 or 40,000 dead Americans" one day soon.

"Al-Qaida has tremendous bench strength," added investigative reporter Peter Lance, author of "1000 Years For Revenge: International Terrorism and the FBI."

"I don't think anybody on this panel will disagree that they're going to hit us again, and therefore, how do we fix the system that hasn't really been fixed since 9-11?"

Scheuer, Lance and others were addressing a gathering of North American television critics. They were promoting a four-hour National Geographic Channel documentary, "Inside 9/11," that will air in August.

The documentary, which draws on newly declassified documents, rarely seen video footage, air-traffic-control tapes and audio recordings made inside the doomed airliners, argues that the U.S. government had many opportunities—stretching back more than a decade—to prevent the attacks.

The Miami Herald (via Knight-Ridder/Tribune News Service), July 18, 2005, pNA.
"The Controversy about U.S. Policies" by Glenn Garvin. © 2005 The Miami Herald.

"I think three presidential administrations are culpable," said Lance, arguing that both Bush presidencies as well as that of Bill Clinton ignored the al-Qaida problem until it was too late. "That's why it's not a political issue, nor is this documentary political. That's what separates it from Michael Moore. . . .

"This is the biggest unsolved homicide in American history, and so far only one individual that we know of has been indicted, Zacarias Moussaoui, a suspected hijacker arrested a month before the attacks. He copped a plea, so we'll never know the full truth."

Lance and Scheuer, who resigned from the CIA last year to protest what he called a cover-up by the government's 9-11 commission, were joined on the panel by Homeland Security aviation-security specialist Bogdan Dzakovic, former New York Fire Department battalion chief Richard Picciotto and *Los Angeles Times* reporter Terry McDermott, whose book "Perfect Soldiers" profiled the Sept. 11 hijackers.

Between them, they hammered just about every aspect of the war on terrorism: Airline security. Mock terrorist teams testing security for the Federal Aviation Administration had proven long before Sept. 11 "that security leaked really bad," said Dzakovic, who worked for the FAA at the time. "We got through security almost all the time with very little problem."

He said his inspectors appealed to the upper echelons of the FAA, as well as to Congress and the White House, to improve security, to no avail. New regulations make it even more difficult to draw attention to security lapses, Dzakovic said: "Federal government whistleblowers engaged in national security work are at an increasing threat from their own government when they bring out problems within the bureaucracy."

Emergency response. Picciotto, who was on the sixth floor of the World Trade Center's North Tower when it collapsed (he was rescued four hours later) said he had ordered the tower evacuated, but the fire department's low-powered radios didn't work—just as they hadn't worked during rescue efforts in a 1993 bombing of the trade center.

The radios still haven't been replaced, Picciotto said: "A lot of families wanted an investigation into why we have faulty radios, and it wasn't addressed."

The FBI. "The FBI does not have an effective computer system to this day," said Lance.

"The day after 9-11, they actually had to Fed Ex the pictures of the 19 hijackers to the 56 regional offices. My 12-year-old could have scanned them and done JPEGs and e-mailed them, and the FBI didn't have that capability." A recent $600-million attempt to upgrade the computers, he said, was a dismal failure.

Foreign policy. Scheuer and McDermott said President Bush and British Prime Minister Tony Blair have falsely portrayed Islamic terrorism as an attack on Western culture rather than as retaliation for U.S. support for Israel and Middle Eastern police states.

"They spent years discussing various political complaints, historical complaints, and very little time at all talking about how evil the West was," said McDermott.

Intelligence reorganization. Scheuer said the much-ballyhooed restructuring of U.S. intelligence under the control of a single czar was useless: "More bureaucracy is never the answer for bad bureaucracy." He said the real problem was the failure of senior CIA officials to act decisively when they had the chance to kill Osama bin Laden.

"My officers afforded this government 10 opportunities to kill bin Laden in '98 and '99. . . . By March of 1999, Bin Laden should have been a smoldering memory," said Scheuer, the author of two best-selling books "Imperial Hubris: Why The West Is Losing The War On Terror" and "Through Our Enemies' Eyes: Osama bin Laden, Radical Islam And The Future Of America"—critical of U.S. policy in the Middle East.

"Did we warn people? Excruciatingly."

17

The USA PATRIOT Act and Civil Liberties

Balancing Civil Liberties and Homeland Security: Does the USA PATRIOT Act Avoid Justice Robert H. Jackson's "Suicide Pact"?

Dick Thornburgh

I. INTRODUCTION

As we commemorate the fiftieth anniversary of the passing of Robert H. Jackson, we honor a man who capitalized on the infinite possibilities a legal education provides. Following his studies at Albany Law School, Justice Jackson's diverse career included serving as a country lawyer in Western New York, a close advisor to President Franklin Delano Roosevelt, Solicitor General and Attorney General of the United States, Justice of the United States Supreme Court, and chief U.S. prosecutor in the Nuremburg trials against Nazi war criminals. Although his career ended over fifty years ago, Jackson, in each of his legal capacities, wrestled with issues that continue to provoke debate in our nation and world today.

A review of Justice Jackson's career reveals his involvement in some of the critical issues with which our country continues to struggle. During his tenure at the Department of Justice, Jackson co-authored briefs and argued the government's position before the United States Supreme Court in cases regarding the constitutionality of the Social Security Act. (1) Today our Congress and President assiduously work to define, or possibly redefine, the role of Social Security and to insure its viability for future generations. Additionally, as a Justice on the United States Supreme Court, Jackson authored the majority

Albany Law Review, Fall 2005, v68, i4, p801(13).

opinion in the case extending First Amendment protection to school children unwilling to salute the American flag. (2) Spirited debate persists today regarding the constitutionality of prayer in public arenas and the use of "God" in the Pledge of Allegiance. Perhaps one of Jackson's most historic statements as a Supreme Court Justice, however, arose from his dissent in Terminiello v. Chicago, (3) where Jackson, drawing on his experience at Nuremburg, argued to uphold a law restricting disorderly conduct and inciting unrest in an effort to preserve order and justice. Clearly, debate regarding the appropriate balance between civil liberties and governmental controls of those liberties is one of the paramount issues we are called upon to face today.

II. THE USA PATRIOT ACT: A MODERN DAY TERMINIELLO?

A. A Brief History of Terminiello v. Chicago

It is often only with the passing of time that we come to appreciate fully the importance of the works of our legal predecessors. At the time of Justice Jackson's dissent in Terminiello, one easily could have viewed his opinion as an inconsequential departure from the majority in an otherwise forgettable case. Jackson's rhetoric, however, now stands for certain hallmark principles in assessing the government's role in preserving civil liberties. The case stems from Father Arthur Terminiello, a suspended Catholic Priest and follower of American fascist leader Gerald L.K. Smith, being found guilty of disorderly conduct in violation of a Chicago city ordinance. Terminiello urged a mob of his sympathizers at a public meeting hall to rise up against a surrounding gathering of his critics. Terminiello warned of the risk of a Communist revolution in the United States, labeled former First Lady Eleanor Roosevelt a Communist, and condemned "atheistic, communistic . . . or Zionist Jews." (4) He referred to the mob of his critics as "slimy scum that got in by mistake." (5) Terminiello's comments incited some members of the audience themselves to make callous remarks about Catholics, Jews, and African Americans, (6) while inciting critics to throw bricks and rocks through the meeting hall windows and break down the auditorium doors. (7) The police experienced difficulty in controlling the mob, but ultimately arrested seventeen individuals and charged Terminiello with provoking the episode. (8)

Justice Douglas, writing for the majority hearing Terminiello's appeal, overturned the conviction, arguing that inviting dispute is a function of the free speech guaranteed by our Constitution. (9) Justice Jackson dissented. In explaining his divergence from Douglas, Jackson wrote: "An old proverb warns us to take heed lest we 'walk into a well from looking at the stars.'" (10) Jackson faulted the Court's majority for considering liberty and order diametric opposites of one another: "This Court seems to regard [liberty and order] as enemies of each other and to be of the view that we must forego order to achieve liberty." (11) Referencing the Nazi conspiracy and aggression with which he was intimately aware, Jackson argued that governments must have the power to control the speech and activity of organized demonstrators and "revolutionary fanatics" or risk being overtaken by terrorist factions; this was the consequence of unchecked factions that arose in pre-World War II Europe. (12) He recognized that while the substance of Terminiello's speech was protected by the First Amendment, Terminiello could not seek constitutional immunity for speech that incited such violence. (13) Jackson concluded his dissent with these historic words: "The choice is not between order and liberty. It is between liberty with order and anarchy without either. There is danger that, if the Court does not temper its doctrinaire logic with a little practical wisdom, it will convert the constitutional Bill of Rights into a suicide pact." (14)

Almost certainly more than any other United States Supreme Court Justice in history, Justice Jackson had a first-hand appreciation of the risk of evil inflicted upon a society by a terrorist faction. Presiding over the Nuremberg trials, Jackson heard actual evidence of genocide and terrorism, and was a witness to the aftermath of a continent being terrorized for over a decade by an organized mob. (15) Jackson had only returned from Nuremberg three years prior to the Terminiello decision, and the lesson of the downfall of the Weimar Republic was foremost in his mind. (16) He understood that civil liberties could only survive under governments with the power to protect those liberties from attack. Recognizing that competing political interests could be fought out through the political system, or "with boots and brass knuckles in the streets," as was the case of the Nazi aggression, (17) Jackson perceived riots as a credible threat to a nation, and had the proof to support his claim.

According to Jackson, the only reason Father Terminiello was able to arrive at the meeting hall, deliver his speech, and escape unharmed was because officers of the law possessed authority to restrain the mob. Order established by law enforcement carved the path for liberty. Quoting Chief Justice Hughes' opinion in Cox v. New Hampshire, Jackson reminded the Court that "[c]ivil liberties, as guaranteed by the Constitution, imply the existence of an organized society maintaining public order without which liberty itself would be lost in the excesses of unrestrained abuses." (18)

B. The USA PATRIOT Act

Although the issues concerning Father Terminiello, including communism and fascism, are not at the forefront of today's news, the extent to which civil liberties should be governed or limited by law continues to be hotly debated. After the horrific terrorist attacks against the United States on September 11,

2001, our country had no choice but to develop new techniques to combat terrorism. Law enforcement and intelligence agencies alike were forced to devise new methods to protect our citizenry and our institutions from the menace of violence and the potential use of weapons of mass destruction against our very homeland. Various governmental entities acknowledged that, historically, cooperation between agencies including law enforcement and intelligence agencies was less than ideal. For example, grand jury testimony and information obtained from court-authorized FBI wiretaps often could not legally be passed on by law enforcement for use by the intelligence community. Likewise, the transmission of intelligence information to law enforcement was frequently inhibited for fear of compromising highly sophisticated electronic surveillance techniques or jeopardizing the lives of under-cover operatives and cooperating witnesses.

Public outrage upon learning that information in the files of one government agency is not fully shared with other agencies is understandable, particularly when the stakes are as high as they inevitably are in both the prevention and prosecution of terrorist activities. Accordingly, a broad national consensus has developed regarding the need to fully empower those to whom we have assigned the task of fighting domestic terrorism. Hearty debate arises, however, when we undertake to determine the exact meaning we should give to the concept of "fully empower."

In an effort to allow more comprehensive intelligence sharing among agencies defending the homeland, Congress passed, by a large margin, the USA PATRIOT Act ("the Act"). (19) Enacted just six weeks after September 11th, the Act sought to remove barriers between various law enforcement and intelligent agencies to provide more effective use of intelligence in fighting terrorism. (20) The Act resulted in a myriad of other changes in the law as well. For example, the Act closed the technology gap in court-authorized electronic surveillance by recognizing the now widespread use of cellular phones and the Internet. (21) The Act also tightened rules for the treatment of an estimated eleven million illegal aliens residing within our borders (22) and extended the reach of money laundering prohibitions to all types of financial service institutions and instruments.

Despite the fact that the Senate passed the USA PATRIOT Act bill 98 to 1 and the House of Representatives passed the bill 357 to 66, much criticism has arisen since its enactment regarding the Act's alleged infringements on civil liberties and other constitutional rights. (23) Some argue that the PATRIOT Act imposes "guilt by association" on aliens by requiring deportation of any alien associated with or endorsing a terrorist organization. (24) Critics also assert that the Act allows the detention of aliens without a hearing or a showing that they pose a threat to national security, both standards below those provided to criminal defendants. (25) Others allege that the Act unfairly amends the Foreign Intelligence Surveillance Act ("FISA"), (26) allowing the issuance of search warrants and wiretaps without probable cause of criminal conducts Detractors theorize that such revision will result in the government using the less restrictive FISA standard to obtain criminal evidence it could not otherwise collect under a probable cause standard. (28)

What is apparently not acknowledged fully by critics of the Act is the crucial distinction that exists between the roles of law enforcement agencies and intelligence gatherers. Law enforcement agencies seek legally admissible evidence to prove a specific criminal offense in court before a judge and jury. Intelligence gatherers, on the other hand, seek information, whether legally admissible or not, to thwart a planned terrorist attack. While information and tactics in these two situations may overlap, they are certainly not the same. The former are designed to punish those who have committed terrorist attacks after the fact, while the latter are designed to prevent terrorist attacks before the fact. While the PATRIOT Act may at times appear to alter the standards of probable cause and sufficiency of evidence, the Act's primary purpose is to prevent further appalling attacks on U.S. citizens, such as those inflicted on September 11th. (29) The fact that evidence obtained under various provisions of the Act might be inadmissible in court should have no bearing, as the intent is to stop terrorist activity from ever taking place. (30)

The consequences of the aforementioned intelligence breakdowns became apparent shortly after the attacks on September 11th. Reports surfaced that several of the hijackers had been previously identified as terrorist threats and were being watched by various government agencies. Sharing of information among law enforcement and intelligence agencies, it is argued, could have thwarted the attacks. Information collected by the CIA and FBI regarding the hijackers did not reach all U.S. law enforcement agencies, resulting in the government's failure to "connect the dots." (31)

As U.S. Attorney General, Jackson struggled with many of the same frustrations in the law. In a lecture to the American Judicature Society in 1941, Jackson called for legislation aimed at controlling the number of illegal aliens within our borders. (32) He noted that, at the time, the United States had over 6,000 deportable aliens, many of whom were criminals and Communists proven to have advocated overthrow of the U.S. government. (33) While outstanding deportation orders existed for these individuals, statutory authority to enforce the orders was absent. (34) Jackson also articulated concerns about foreign agents, arrested for acts against our nation, who were released on bail and returned to American society. (35)

Further, Jackson urged legislation permitting the monitoring and intercepting of telegrams between saboteurs, explaining to the Judicature Society that "[t]he wires of America today are a protected communication system for the enemies of America." (36) As an example, Jackson pointed to the sabotage of U.S. ships in U.S. ports ordered via telegrams sent to the ships' masters. (37) He argued that "carefully limited legislation" would allow the government forewarning of enemy attacks, while still respecting privacy of the mails and wires. (38) Jackson warned his audience that efforts to strengthen law enforcement would be obstructed by critics, but challenged the Judicature

Society and the Bar to nevertheless effect the necessary changes to the law. (39)

Today, our constitutional Bill of Rights faces the same risk of becoming a "suicide pact" as it did in 1949 when Justice Jackson wrestled with Terminiello. If our government does not enact laws necessary to surveil for dangers and protect our democracy, our Bill of Rights could lose all meaning. If true freedom and liberty are to continue to be realized, our government must be permitted to exercise adequate powers in protecting them. Unlimited freedom of speech, privacy, or entry across our borders will be of little benefit when terrorists invade our homeland.

Our world as we knew it changed on that frightful morning in September 2001. Our vulnerability to terrorists who despise our way of life became apparent. We must now, as a nation, act affirmatively to protect our democracy. While debate regarding the role our government should have in our lives inevitably will continue, Jackson's "suicide pact" principle holds true. We can only enjoy genuine liberty alongside the existence of order; eroding order for the sake of unlimited civil liberties will result in a terrorist triumph.

In the wake of September 11th and the enactment of the PATRIOT Act, evidence illustrates success in striking a balance between homeland security and civil liberties. In 2004, Utah Senator Orrin Hatch praised the ability of the PATRIOT Act to effectuate justice without eroding civil liberties. Senator Hatch stated that the Justice Department's Inspector General reported, in three consecutive semi-annual reports, that it had received "absolutely no complaints" alleging misconduct by Justice Department employees in their application of the substantive provisions of the PATRIOT Act. (40) This is due, in part no doubt, to provisions of the Act that provide additional protection to civil rights by allowing recovery for willful violations of the law (41) and requiring judicial oversight of certain investigations. (42) If abuses occur in the future, however, they will be treated similarly to the misuse of any other law, resulting in suppression of evidence, reversals of convictions, and damages awarded for misconduct. (43)

As portions of the PATRIOT Act approach sunset on December 31, 2005, controversial provisions will likely be subject to legislative effort at amendment. Although unable to document any specific abuse of its provisions, the Patriots to Restore Checks and Balances, a broad coalition of advocates made up of public interest groups and former Members of Congress, has stated they will seek to focus on three provisions of the Act they claim are inimical to the exercise of civil rights and liberties: the so-called "sneak and peek" searches by federal agents without the requirement of instant notification; the availability of records from institutions such as libraries, gun shops, and medical offices; and the use of an overly broad definition of "terrorism" in pursuing suspects. (44) Despite its qualms, the coalition agrees that the PATRIOT Act is a necessary tool for defeating terrorism. (45) Current Members of Congress will also introduce legislation aimed at reducing the scope of the Act. (46) Responding to criticisms, Attorney General Alberto R. Gonzales stated before the Senate Judiciary Committee that while he invites ideas for improving the PATRIOT Act provisions due to sunset in 2005, he adamantly urges making all of these provisions permanent, as they are indispensable tools for fighting terrorism and serious crime. (47)

Former Attorney General John Ashcroft also recently testified before the Senate Judiciary Committee, stressing the significance of protections the PATRIOT Act provides. Ashcroft stated, "al Qaeda has a fanatical desire to wage war on Americans in America. Al Qaeda will send terrorist soldier after terrorist soldier to infiltrate our borders and to melt into our communities. And they do not wear uniforms. They do not respect human rights. They target civilians." (48) If we fail to provide our government with effective tools to seek out terrorists and bring them to justice, our way of life will be degraded once again as it was on September 11th.

Chief Justice William H. Rehnquist has also weighed in on the issue of liberty versus order and, like Jackson, arrived at conclusions similar to those discussed herein in light of the PATRIOT Act. The Chief Justice argued that civil liberties can only truly be protected by a government with power to maintain order among its people: It is not simply 'liberty' but civil liberty of which we speak. The word 'civil,' in turn, is derived from the Latin word civis, which means 'citizen.' A citizen is a person owing allegiance to some organized government, and not a person in an idealized 'state of nature' free from any governmental restraint. Judge Learned Hand, in remarks entitled 'The Spirit of Liberty,' delivered during World War II, put it this way: 'A society in which men recognize no check upon their freedom soon becomes a society where freedom is the possession of only a savage few. . . .' (49)

In conflicts between individual liberty and governmental authority, Rehnquist noted, individual liberty will not always prevail. (50) One can imagine Justice Jackson penning the following, also written by Justice Rehnquist: "In wartime, reason and history both suggest that [the balance between freedom and order] shifts to some degree in favor of order—in favor of the government's ability to deal with conditions that threaten the national well-being." (51)

C. Justice Jackson: A Common Sense Perspective

If Justice Jackson were alive today, he would warn us that it is more important now more than ever that the United States take decisive steps to prevent our Constitution from becoming the "suicide pact" he referred to in the Terminiello case. Terror, and the threat of terror, is alive in historic proportions. Jackson would advise that we need to prevent our cherished freedoms from falling into the hands of a savage few. He would point us to the horrors of terrorism and genocide in Nazi Germany, the evidence of which he was intimately familiar and the proponents of which he prosecuted. As Jackson once wrote, "Mussolini, Hitler, Stalin, and lesser imitators rejected the process of out-arguing and out-voting adversaries and have forcibly seized power, suppressed liberties and set up dictatorships." (52) If he were drafting this passage today, Jackson surely would add al Qaeda and Osama bin Laden's names to the list. Justice Jackson would view the PATRIOT Act for what it is—a necessary and common sense means to protect our system of democracy and organized government. But he would do so with a sense of fairness and recognition of the importance of the presumption of innocence. Prior to the commencement of the Nuremberg trials, Jackson fiercely negotiated for a presumption of innocence with U.S.S.R. prosecutor General Ion T. Nikitchenko, who argued that Nazi defendants should be presumed guilty. (53) Jackson's presumption of innocence argument prevailed only after he threatened Nikitchenko that the U.S. would not otherwise participate in the trials. (54) Again recognizing that liberty and order must operate in tandem, Jackson remarked in his opening statement at the trials, "[t]o pass these defendants a poisoned chalice is to put it to our own lips as well." (55) This standard of guilt resulted in the acquittal of three Nazi defendants. (56)

While Jackson would recognize the rights of individuals under the PATRIOT Act, he would have stern words for the Act's critics. He would remind them of the old proverb he cited in Terminiello: "take heed lest we walk into a well from looking at the stars." Jackson would argue that while certain methods of implementing such safeguards may have the real or perceived effects of limiting civil liberties, we cannot pretend that our civil liberties are constant or that they reside in a vacuum. Justice Jackson knew that it is not a choice between liberty and order, but a choice between liberty with order or anarchy without either. In response to critics of the Nuremberg trials, Jackson wrote, "[f]riends of liberty will find grim instruction in the rise of the Nazi party, its methods of seizure of power, and its establishment of dictatorial control over the German people." (57) While our civil liberties may not be absolute under the PATRIOT Act, our liberties could become non-existent without it. A society that presumes innocence in a court of law while aggressively pursuing evidence of planned bad acts will remain stable.

III. CONCLUSION

Eugene Gerhart, the sole biographer of Robert H. Jackson, once said, "[l]ike President Ronald Reagan, Jackson operated on principles, not on the basis of public opinion polls." (58) Jackson understood that, while not always popular, striking a balance between civil liberties and government order is of paramount importance. As U.S. Prosecutor at Nuremberg, Jackson wrote to President Truman: "The legal position which the United States will maintain, being thus based on the common sense of justice, is relatively simple and non-technical." (59) Jackson carried this philosophy with him throughout his career—as advocate, prosecutor, defender, and judge—recognizing that a common sense balance of power and liberty promotes democracy and stability.

Dick Thornburgh, Counsel, Kirkpatrick & Lockhart Nicholson Graham LLP, Washington, DC. Mr. Thornburgh served as Attorney General of the United States under Presidents Ronald Reagan and George H.W. Bush (1988–1991). Mr. Thornburgh gratefully acknowledges Eric C. Rusnak, an associate at Kirkpatrick & Lockhart Nicholson Graham LLP, for his contributions to this work.

NOTES

(1) See Steward Machine Co. v. Davis, 301 U.S. 548 (1937) (upholding Social Security's unemployment compensation system); Helvering v. Davis, 301 U.S. 619 (1937) (upholding Social Security's old age pension system).

(2) See W. Va. State Bd. of Educ. v. Barnette, 319 U.S. 624 (1943).

(3) 337 U.S, 1, 13 (1949) (Jackson, J., dissenting).

(4) Id. at 17-20 (Jackson, J., dissenting).

(5) Id. at 17 (Jackson, J., dissenting).

(6) Id. at 22 (Jackson, J., dissenting).

(7) Id. at 16 (Jackson, J., dissenting).

(8) Id. (Jackson, J., dissenting).

(9) Id. at 4.

(10) Id. at 14 (Jackson, J., dissenting).

(11) Id. (Jackson, J., dissenting).

(12) Id. at 23-24 (Jackson, J., dissenting). Jackson, quoting *Mein Kampf,* wrote: We should not work in secret conventicles, but in mighty mass demonstrations, and it is not by dagger and poison or pistol that the road can be cleared for the movement but by the conquest of the streets. We must teach the Marxists that the future master of the streets is National Socialism, just as it will some day be the master of the state. Id. (Jackson, J., dissenting).

(13) Id. at 25 (Jackson, J., dissenting).

(14) Id. at 37 (Jackson, J., dissenting). It appears that Justice Jackson first used the term "suicide pact" in an unpublished draft opinion in Hirabayashi v. United States, a case assessing the power of the U.S. Army to impose a curfew on United States citizens of Japanese ancestry during World War II. "Nothing in the Constitution requires it to be construed as a suicide pact. It recognized the existence of a war power which it does not define or expressly limit." Dennis J. Hutchinson, "The Achilles Heel" of the Constitution: Justice Jackson and the Japanese Exclusion Cases, 2002 SUP. CT. REV. 455, 463 (2002) (quoting Undated draft, Box 128, RHJP). Ultimately, Jackson's opinion was not published. Id. The term "suicide pact" was later quoted by Justice Arthur Goldberg in Kennedy v. Mendoza-Martinez, 372 U.S. 144, 160 (1963). Assessing the citizenship rights of draft evaders, Goldberg theorized "It]he powers of Congress to require military service for the common defense are broad and far-reaching, for while the Constitution protects against invasions of individual rights, it is not a suicide pact." 372 U.S. at 159-60. The Mendoza-Martinez decision tends to be more frequently cited than Terminiello for the term "suicide pact," possibly because it was the majority opinion. Nevertheless, Justice Jackson had employed the phrase fourteen years earlier.

(15) See WILLIAM H. REHNQUIST, ALL THE LAWS BUT ONE: CIVIL LIBERTIES IN WARTIME 195 (1998) (noting that Justice Jackson's experiences as United

States prosecutor at the Nuremberg trials "had a profound effect on his judicial philosophy").

(16) GLENDON SCHUBERT, DISPASSIONATE JUSTICE: A SYNTHESIS OF THE JUDICIAL OPINIONS OF ROBERT H. JACKSON 89 (1969).

(17) Id.

(18) Terminiello v. Chicago, 337 U.S. 1, 31 (1949) (Jackson, J., dissenting). Jackson also referred to this balance between liberty and rule of law as "the oft-forgotten principle . . . that freedom of speech exists only under law and not independently of it." Id. (Jackson, J., dissenting).

(19) Uniting and Strengthening America by Providing Appropriate Tools Required to Intercept and Obstruct Terrorism Act of 2001, Pub. L. No. 107-56, 115 Stat. 272 (2001).

(20) For a discussion of the barriers the PATRIOT Act seeks to eliminate, see Craig S. Lerner, The USA PATRIOT Act: Promoting the Cooperation of Foreign Intelligence Gathering and Law Enforcement, 11 GEO. MASON L. REV. 493 (2003); see also Counterterrorism Technology and Privacy: Report on the Cantigny Conference, 27 A.B.A NAT'L SECURITY L. REP. 4-5 (2005) (noting that international threats to national security and domestic threats from terrorists are no longer distinguishable) [hereinafter Counterterrorism Technology and Privacy].

(21) See generally Orin S. Kerr, Internet Surveillance Law After the USA PATRIOT Act: The Big Brother That Isn't, 97 NW. U. L. REV. 607 (2003) (discussing changes to electronic surveillance laws and arguing that the PATRIOT Act does not significantly encroach upon electronic privacy expectations, as common wisdom might suggest).

(22) See generally Lawrence M. Lebowitz & Ira L. Podheiser, A Summary of the Changes in Immigration Policies and Practices After the Terrorist Attacks of September 11, 2001: The USA PATRIOT Act and Other Measures, 63 U. PITT L. REV. 873 (2002) (outlining various shifts in immigration laws and policies as a result of the September 11th terrorist attacks).

(23) While some believe that the PATRIOT Act was rushed through Congress, the Act reflects the drafters' concerns in balancing civil liberties and national security. See Viet D. Dinh, How the USA PATRIOT Act Defends Democracy, 2 GEO. J. L. & PUB. POL'Y 393, 394 (2004).

(24) David Cole, Enemy Aliens, 54 STAN. L, REV. 953, 966-70 (2002).

(25) Id. at 970-71.

(26) 50 U.S.C. [subsection] 1801 1863 (2000).

(27) See Cole, supra note 24, at 973. This criticism misconstrues the law in that the issuance of warrants for wiretaps and other surveillance without a showing of probable cause of criminal conduct is only permitted if the foreign power or its agent is a non-U.S, individual. Even in those instances, government officers still must show that there is probable cause to believe the target of the surveillance is a foreign power or an agent of a foreign power and that each of the facilities or places to be monitored are being used or are about to be used by the foreign power or its agent. 50 U.S.C. [section] 1805 (a)(3) (2000). If the agent is of a foreign power is a U.S. person, the element of criminality must be present. Id. [section] 1801 (b)(2)(A)-(E). This system allows the government to monitor foreign powers and their agents without impinging upon the rights of U.S. persons.

(28) Cole, supra note 24, at 973-74.

(29) Justice Jackson offered a similar analysis in his dissent in Korematsu v. United States, 323 U.S. 214, 242 (1944) (Jackson, J., dissenting), one of the Japanese internment cases. Scrutinizing the constitutionality of a military order excluding, for security reasons, all persons of Japanese ancestry from a certain area, he said: "In the very nature of things,

military decisions are not susceptible of intelligent judicial appraisal. They do not pretend to rest on evidence, but are made on information that often would not be admissible and on assumptions that could not be proved." Id. at 245 (Jackson, J., dissenting). Although Jackson ultimately believed the military exclusion order was unconstitutional, his reasoning here shows his recognition that security measures do not always have to follow principles of criminal law and evidentiary procedure.

(30) See Counterterrorism Technology and Privacy, supra note 20, at 5 (explaining that the role of law enforcement personnel is to look backward to reconstruct a crime, while the role of intelligence personnel is to look forward, usually covertly, to prevent a crime).

(31) Lerner, supra note 20, at 493.

(32) See Robert H. Jackson, Put Law of National Defense in Order, 25 J. AM. JUDICA-TURE SOC'Y 6, 9 (1941–1942).

(33) Id.

(34) Id.

(35) Id.

(36) Id. Jackson advocated strongly for the power to monitor and prevent the transmission of terrorist threats through the mails and wires: "Must we not only allow foreign attacks on our policy but also carry it for them in our mails?" Id.

(37) Id. at 9.

(38) See id.

(39) Id.

(40) Federal Government Counterterrorism Efforts: Hearing of the Senate Judiciary Comm, 108th Cong. (2004) (opening statement of Sen. Orrin G. Hatch, Chairman, Senate Comm. on Judiciary) [hereinafter Federal Government Counterterrorism Efforts]. See Joseph G. Poluka, The PATRIOT Act: Indispensable Tool Against Terror, 76 PA. BAR ASS'N. Q. 33, 38 (2005) (stating that the warnings of abuses from implementing the PATRIOT Act "simply have not been realized"); Beryl A. Howell, Surveillance Powers in the USA PATRIOT Act: How Scary are They?, 76 PA. BAR ASS'N. Q. 12, 13-14 (discussing certain myths about the PATRIOT Act, including the facts behind accusations that Congress "rubber stamped" the Administration's request for the Act, that Congress "short-circuited" the normal legislative process, and that the Act is responsible for a multitude of contentious civil liberties actions taken by the Bush Administration).

(41) See Oversight of the USA PATRIOT Act: Hearing of the Senate Judiciary Comm, 109th Cong. (2005) (statement of Attorney General Alberto R. Gonzales) (noting that Section 223 of the Act provides for monetary damages for willful violation of the criminal wiretap statute) [hereinafter Oversight o/the USA PATRIOT Act].

(42) See id. (discussing Sections 201, 202, 206, 209, 214, 215, and 220, all of which require some degree of court approval for wiretaps and search warrants).

(43) See Peluka, supra note 40, at 38.

(44) See Eric Lichtblau, Coalition Forms to Oppose Parts of Antiterrorism Law, N.Y. TIMES, Mar. 23, 2005, at A10. See also Howell, supra note 40, at 19 (noting that courts, including the U.S. Supreme Court, have sanctioned "sneak and peek" warrants for over a decade); Andrew C. McCarthy, Spinning the PATRIOT Act: Sneaking a Peek at "'Judge" Napolitano's Latest Debacle, NAT'L REV. ONLINE, available at http://www.nationalreview.com/mccarthy/mccarthy 200504070805.asp (noting widespread misconceptions of "sneak and peek" searches, including former New Jersey Superior Court Judge Andrew Napolitano's mischaracterization of this provision on the April 4, 2005 edition of The O'Reilly Factor, alleging, incorrectly, that FBI agents can conduct "sneak and peek" searches by using self-written warrants that permit them "to

break into your house and make it look like a burglary" and "steal your checkbook" or "plant a chip in your computer"). In actuality, "sneak and peek" warrants, or delayed-notice search warrants, can only be issued by a federal judge and only upon a showing of probable cause that the property to be searched or seized constitutes evidence of a criminal offense. Delayed-notice warrants differ from normal search warrants only in that a judge specifically authorizes law enforcement to wait a limited time before notifying the subject of the search that the warrant has been executed. See 18 U.S.C. [section] 3103(a) & (b).

(45) See Lichtblau, supra note 44, at A10.

(46) See Dan Eggen, Patriot Act Changes to Be Proposed, WASH. POST, Apr. 5, 2005, at A21.

(47) See Oversight of the USA PATRIOT Act, supra note 41 (statement of Attorney General Alberto R. Gonzales).

(48) Federal Government Counterterrorism Efforts, supra note 40 (statement of Attorney General John Ashcroft).

(49) REHNQUIST, supra note 15, at 222 (citation omitted).

(50) See id. at 222–23.

(51) Id. at 222. See also Robert H. Jackson, Wartime Security and Liberty Under Law, 1 BUFF. L. REV. 103, 104 (1951) (noting: "Freedom is achieved only by a complex but just structure of rules of law, impersonally and dispassionately enforced against both rules and the governed.").

(52) Robert H. Jackson, Liberty Under Law, Address Before the New York State Bar Association (Jan. 30, 1954), at www.roberthjackson.org/Man/Libertyunderlaw/.

(53) See Henry T. King, Jr., Robert Jackson's Transcendent Influence Over Today's World, 68 ALB. L. REV. 23, 26 (2004); see also Robert H. Jackson, Justice Jackson's Report to President Truman on the Legal Basis for Trial of War Criminals, 19 TEMP. L.Q. 144, 148 (1945–46) [hereinafter Justice Jackson's Report to President Truman] ("But undiscriminating executions or punishments [of the alleged war criminals] without definite findings of guilt, fairly arrived at, would ... not set easily on the American conscience or be remembered by our children with pride."); Robert H. Jackson, Justice Jackson Weighs Nuremberg's Lessons, N.Y. TIMES MAG., June 16, 1946, at 12 (arguing that without trying the alleged Nazi criminals, the United States could be likened to Nazis executing political enemies without a hearing).

(54) See King, supra note 53, at 26. Jackson was cognizant of the fact that the Nuremberg trials provided the accused with a liberty unavailable under their former regime. In his closing remarks at Nuremberg, Jackson said: "History will know that whatever could be said, [the defendants] were allowed to say. They have been given the kind of trial which they, in the days of their pomp and power, never gave to any man." Robert H. Jackson, Closing Arguments for Conviction of Nazi War Criminals, 20 TEMP. L.Q. 85, 85 (1946–47).

(55) Opening Statement for the United States of America by Robert H. Jackson, Chief of Counsel for the United States at the Palace of Justice, Nurnberg, Germany, November 21, 1945, reprinted in ROBERT H. JACKSON, THE NURNBERG CASE 30, 34 (1947).

(56) See King, supra note 53, at 26.

(57) Justice Jackson Weighs Nuremberg's Lessons, supra note 53, at 60.

(58) Eugene C. Gerhart, The Legacy of Robert H. Jackson, 68 ALB. L. REV. 19, 20 (2004).

(59) Justice Jackson's Report to President Truman,, supra note 53, at 152.

InfoMarks: Make Your Mark

What Is an InfoMark?

It is a single-click return ticket to any page, any result, or any search from InfoTrac College Edition.

An InfoMark is a stable URL, linked to InfoTrac College Edition articles that you have selected. InfoMarks can be used like any other URL, but they're better because they're stable—they don't change. Using an InfoMark is like performing the search again whenever you follow the link, whether the result is a single article or a list of articles.

How Do InfoMarks Work?

If you can "copy and paste," you can use InfoMarks.

When you see the InfoMark icon on a result page, its URL can be copied and pasted into your electronic document—web page, word processing document, or email. Once InfoMarks are incorporated into a document, the results are persistent (the URLs will not change) and are dynamic.

Even though the saved search is used at different times by different users, an InfoMark always functions like a brand new search. Each time a saved search is executed, it accesses the latest updated information. That means subsequent InfoMark searches might yield additional or more up-to-date information than the original search with less time and effort.

Capabilities

InfoMarks are the perfect technology tool for creating:

- Virtual online readers
- Current awareness topic sites—links to periodical or newspaper sources
- Online/distance learning courses
- Bibliographies, reference lists
- Electronic journals and periodical directories
- Student assignments
- Hot topics

Advantages

- Select from over 15 million articles from more than 5,000 journals and periodicals
- Update article and search lists easily
- Articles are always full-text and include bibliographic information
- All articles can be viewed online, printed, or emailed
- Saves professors and students time
- Anyone with access to InfoTrac College Edition can use it
- No other online library database offers this functionality
- FREE!

How to Use InfoMarks

There are three ways to utilize InfoMarks—in HTML documents, Word documents, and Email

HTML Document

1. Open a new document in your HTML editor (Netscape Composer or FrontPage Express).
2. Open a new browser window and conduct your search in InfoTrac College Edition.
3. Highlight the URL of the results page or article that you would like to InfoMark.
4. Right-click the URL and click Copy. Now, switch back to your HTML document.
5. In your document, type in text that describes the InfoMarked item.
6. Highlight the text and click on Insert, then on Link in the upper bar menu.
7. Click in the link box, then press the "Ctrl" and "V" keys simultaneously and click OK. This will paste the URL in the box.
8. Save your document.

Word Document

1. Open a new Word document.
2. Open a new browser window and conduct your search in InfoTrac College Edition.
3. Check items you want to add to your Marked List.
4. Click on Mark List on the right menu bar.
5. Highlight the URL, right-click on it, and click Copy. Now, switch back to your Word document.
6. In your document, type in text that describes the InfoMarked item.
7. Highlight the text. Go to the upper bar menu and click on Insert, then on Hyperlink.

8. Click in the hyperlink box, then press the "Ctrl" and "V" keys simultaneously and click OK. This will paste the URL in the box.
9. Save your document.

Email

1. Open a new email window.
2. Open a new browser window and conduct your search in InfoTrac College Edition.
3. Highlight the URL of the results page or article that you would like to InfoMark.
4. Right-click the URL and click Copy. Now, switch back to your email window.
5. In the email window, press the "Ctrl" and "V" keys simultaneously. This will paste the URL into your email.
6. Send the email to the recipient. By clicking on the URL, he or she will be able to view the InfoMark.